2007 — 28 yrs old.

Bit more certainty a
confidence about my
life, despite the recent
trials. Am engaged to
be married in 2008, so
can see a more stable
life ahead of me.

<u>2014</u>

The Butterfly Experience:
Inspiration For Change

The Butterfly Experience: Inspiration For Change

Karen Whitelaw Smith

First edition
Published in Great Britain

By Mirage Publishing 2007
Text Copyright © Karen Whitelaw Smith 2007
First published in paperback 2007

A CIP catalogue record for this book
Is available from the British Library.

ISBN: 978-1-90257-826-2

Mirage Publishing
PO Box 161
Gateshead
NE8 4WW
Great Britain

Printed and bound in Great Britain by

Forward Press
Remus House, Coltsfoot Drive, Woodston, Peterborough, PE2 9JX

Cover logo © Elmwood Design Ltd

Papers used in the production of this book are recycled,
thus reducing environmental depletion.

To my loving father, John W Syme, who died on 25 October 2000 from prostate cancer. A private man, his hugely positive influence inspired this book.

Foreword

Most people would say I am a very lucky man. I have a beautiful wife and three fabulous kids. I run an internationally acclaimed brand design business, which allows me to interact with the most stimulating men and women around. I'm the proud recipient of an honorary doctorate.

Let's look at the same glass from the half-empty perspective. My life has been a constant challenge. I struggled terribly at school, teased mercilessly due to chronic eczema. I failed my eleven-plus and left secondary school with just three grade 'C' O-levels. At the age of twenty-eight, a dinner party guest guessed my age at forty-two!

That's my life, seen from two completely different perspectives. For the most part, and this is my *real* fortune, I choose a positive viewpoint. I never see a problem as a problem. It's just an obstacle that I have to navigate. Challenges are part of life's 'seasoning'. Without them how can we calibrate or enjoy the good times? And there *are* lots of good times, if we choose to see them that way.

Some of the happiest people I know don't have the benefits of affluent lifestyles, yet they enjoy every moment of every day. They don't just see their glass as half-full; instead they're grateful for the half they've already drunk.

I guess if you're reading this book you're looking for some kind of transition; perhaps when you look at *your* glass you're seeing the contents just drain away. If so, take heart. Karen's book offers both encouragement *and* practical tools to help you find a more positive way forward. Keep an open mind. Enjoy the journey. I promise you've taken the first step to a happier, more fulfilling future.

Jonathan Sands
Chairman, Elmwood Design Ltd.

Member, Wal-mart Strategy Council

Note to the Reader

Dear Reader,

All my life I've been drawn to butterflies. I love their variety, their colours and their delicate strength. I call them my 'Butterfly Blessings'.

There's an old saying that butterflies are drawn to healers; they've sought me out all my life. Sitting recently in a packed auditorium, a beautiful Monarch butterfly flew onto my shoulder. I asked it to fly to my hand. It stayed there for quite some time, allowing me to stroke its wings. When I whispered it was free to go it flew off - with some hesitation. The beautiful creature circled me for some time before disappearing.

The butterfly is the perfect symbol for this book. It represents hope, happiness and lightness of being. Some say it's a sign of faith released. It's easy to forget that the butterfly's beauty has come at great cost. Throughout its journey it has undergone profound transformations and survived many obstacles.

We are like butterflies, constantly changing and growing. At times our lives can *seem* full of hardship. So I've written *The Butterfly Experience* to tell you it doesn't have to be that way. I want *The Butterfly Experience* to give you the magic ingredient for a successful, happy life. It's called belief: we have to *believe* we can change. My techniques are designed to anchor that belief. They'll help you overcome fear so you can *finally* be who you deserve to be. I want to help you break out of your safe cocoon and experience personal freedom. I want you to stretch yourself by using the techniques and lessons I've been using for many years. They're guaranteed to help you grow - *if* you're prepared to commit to change. This Experience will enhance and enrich your life in ways you can't even begin to imagine. If the Monarch butterfly, a tiny, fragile creature, can fly thousands of miles to its winter resting place, what could *you* achieve?

Just like the butterfly, you already have everything you need for the journey within you. You've begun a process which will lead you to a life of joy and abundance. These are no empty promises. They have become manifest in my life and in the lives of my patients. They can become real for you too. This is your chance to fly.

I know some of you may be feeling sceptical. So here's a challenge. Read *The Butterfly Experience*. Apply the techniques for thirty days. Your life will change.

It's time. Time to be positive about what you want from life. Time to use your mind to achieve the results you want. Time to become responsible for your own happiness. Today's thoughts create your tomorrow. You *can* change. *The Butterfly Experience* has begun. It's time to live your life and love your life.

Butterfly Blessings!

Karen

Anything Can Happen If You Let It

Sometimes things are difficult, but you can bet it
Doesn't have to be so, changes can be made
You can move a mountain if you use a larger spade
Anything can happen it's a marvel
You can be a butterfly, or just stay larval
Stretch your mind beyond fantastic
Dreams are made of – strong elastic
Take some sound advice and don't forget it
Anything can happen if you let it

George Stiles & Anthony Drewe

Contents

FINDING OUT WHO YOU ARE

GROWING PAINS

GOING WITHIN

LEARNING TO FLY

INTRODUCTION

This book was written for everyone who finds it difficult to accept change. I was once that person. After years of developing my own techniques, I want to offer you the chance to change your life for the better. Today I am in control of my life and my destiny. I know where I'm going. I understand my purpose. I'm here to help others find an easier path through life, to show how to live a life of abundance.

There is nobody this book would not benefit. But I've written it for YOU. It is intended to be practical and inspirational. Each section will provide you with tried and tested techniques for self-relaxation, visualisation, goal setting and energy work. You'll benefit most by working through the book from beginning to end, working through the exercises and practicing the techniques as you go. This is not a programme you can cherry pick through. It should be worked in chronological order. Don't try and skip ahead. Or is that what you think life is all about?

I want you to get maximum benefit from the work and I want that benefit to start today! I want you to enjoy your life as much as I enjoy mine. If you are willing to commit to change then you're half way there. Using my seven secret solutions you'll be amazed how quickly your life starts to turn around.

CAUTION

In *The Butterfly Experience*, not everyone makes it through to flight. Some of you will become glorious butterflies. Some will hold on to fear and remain locusts – living in turmoil. This book is not a magic wand. It requires discipline. Spiritual discipline. It's *believing* that makes it magic.

You are a seeker. You may already have tried courses, therapies and training. You may have wasted money and achieved nothing. My techniques are free. You can do them from home. I even give you a guarantee that they will work. All I ask is that you start to bring some discipline into your life; practice, practice, practice. You'll soon see mind-blowing results.

Locust or Butterfly? Which will *you* be?

There is a *Butterfly Journal* at the back of this book which enables you to record your personal journey of self-discovery. Journaling will help you to keep a record of where you are and how far you have progressed.

Author's note: All case histories in this book are true. Names have been changed to protect patient privacy.

FINDING OUT WHO YOU ARE

1

You Can Be A Butterfly, Or Just Stay Larval

Waiting for the miracle that will make you happy? Fed up looking to other people for approval? Ever wish your life had come with a set of instructions?

Well, now it does! Welcome to *The Butterfly Experience*!

The book you're holding will give you the guidance you've been waiting for.

It's going to show you how to take control of your destiny. It will teach you how to stop making the same mistakes time after time. It will help you make conscious choices that will lead you to success and happiness.

With proven ideas, techniques, tips and solutions, *The Butterfly Experience* is the key to a healthy, happy and abundant life.

You know that feeling when you want the world to stop so you can get off and just *think*? *The Butterfly Experience* offers you that chance. Even better - it offers a *new* way of thinking about WHO you are, WHERE you're going and WHAT you want out of life. Today is the day you stop bumbling through life, getting swept up by other people's agendas. To be truly happy you have to get to know the truth about who you are.

The closest most people get to being truly happy is daydreaming. Instead of focusing on what we want and how to get it, we make the classic mistake that *guarantees we stay right where we are*. We concentrate on what we *don't* want. By giving our energy to the negative we attract it. We struggle at the mercy of our emotions. Above all we allow ourselves to feel like victims. There's tremendous power in that mindset – victims don't need to change. So negative thinking becomes an engrained habit.

Negative thinking harms us. Negative thinking is the root cause of disease. Negative thinking draws negative people and experiences into our lives. Yet we *still* insist on doing it! So how do we *stop* being casualties of our own thinking? The *real* question is…how motivated are you to *change*?

'If you can dream it, you can do it'

Walt Disney

With a positive mindset we can achieve anything we set out to do. But first we have to conquer the enemy within – our own negativity. If ignorance or fear has been your excuse up till now, here's a warning. They're officially no longer valid! It's time to get honest here. No more lies. No more self-deceit. The truth about who you are and what you want is about to become the springboard that will catapult you into the life you deserve.

Life is simple. Every new day presents us with choices and challenges. How we cope with them dictates the quality of our lives. The secret to success isn't elusive; we have to know what we want, work hard for it and persist when things get tough. Yet we keep on making the same mistakes, looking for a different outcome. We refuse to abandon the comfort of our old thinking, our cocoon, for fear of trying something new. The procrastinating is over. That's just a big word for 'fear'. No one likes change, but without it nothing changes. So open yourself up to this process, welcome it, embrace it. Follow the directions in this book and watch the magic happen.

Butterflies are quite different from all other creatures on the planet. To evolve they undergo a series of profound, miraculous changes. This book is all about change – why we need it, how to do it and how to make that process as painless and as enriching as possible. *The Butterfly Experience* is full of meditations, creative exercises, positive healing and new thinking which will awaken your spirit. I want you to live life consciously, to be alive to its possibilities and wonders. At the end of this process I want you to rise majestically to the life you deserve, vibrant and unique.

Butterflies emerge from their cocoons as captivating, joyous creatures. But this 'flying flower' has transformed itself completely, going through four separate stages of change. Each stage has a different goal. Each has a different set of obstacles which must be overcome if the butterfly is to survive. Our lives – if they are to be lives worth living – undergo similar metamorphoses. Each phase of our journey should bring us closer to our goal. But first you have to believe that change is possible. You have to *believe* you're entitled to happiness.

The first stage in the butterfly's life cycle is the 'Egg'. Not the most glamorous of titles, I'll grant you, but it's our starting point. We humans start life as an egg. The egg is the symbol of life – the great gift we all receive. The appropriate response to any gift – especially one so precious – is gratitude. And that's where I want us to begin. I want you to reflect for a moment on your life. Consider all you've been through, the lessons you've learned, the people who've helped you along the way. Be grateful for the wisdom you have today. Fundamentally we're all the same – we have a universality of thoughts and emotions. But the standards and values *you* bring to *The Butterfly Experience* are your unique gifts to this process. I want to help you recognise them and learn to live by them always. Let's begin...

Each butterfly egg is laid in a protected place. Hopefully our families allowed us shelter from life's harms. Butterfly eggs – just like us – come in different colours, shapes and sizes. Each egg is surrounded by a hard outer shell, which protects the new life inside. It's called the *chorion*. I like to think of it as the face or mask we develop, the false identity that shelters our egos. All you need for this new beginning is the tiniest of cracks in this protective outer shell. A tiny change in your thinking. Just enough to let in new light, a chink in your armour.

Is it possible for you to admit that there may be more to learn? It's time to ask your Self

ARE YOU READY TO TAKE CONTROL OF YOUR LIFE?

If the answer is 'yes' you've hit the jackpot, because I'm here to give you a 'how to'. I'm going to teach you simple techniques which will help you be happy, healthy, have bundles of energy and enjoy an overflow of abundance. It's time to get in the driving seat of your own life. Instead of being spoon fed happiness, or taking it at someone else's expense – why not create it? Success is not a matter of luck, it's a reward.

Each new butterfly's life depends for sustenance on what's already inside it. The same applies to us on our journeys. When the chips are down, all we have are the resources within. In *The Butterfly Experience* our first job is to identify those resources – what strengths we have, what unique qualities we possess, what's happening inside us, today. This first stage of *The Butterfly Experience* will identify your untapped resources. It will provide the means for you to grow, spiritually and emotionally.

Of course the butterfly has it easier to a degree. It is following a predetermined path. In order for you to rise up you'll need to find *your* path. So it's time to face facts. Whenever life isn't going according to plan, it's because we don't *have* a plan! That's about to change. You are about to begin creating an individual plan for your life. *The Butterfly Experience* is designed specifically to enable you to do that.

Remember - it's for you and you alone. No more cobbling together ideas based on other people's ideas of contentment. No more worrying about the expectations of family or the 'needs' of friends. It's only by looking inside of ourselves, by becoming conscious of our own thoughts, that we start to grow. Soon *you* will decide what to think and feel. *You'll* decide what ideas to accept or reject. *You'll* control your body. Most importantly, after reading *The Butterfly Experience* you'll never again wonder why you're here. I'm not talking about the job you have, or the relationship you're in. I'm talking about knowing the reason you *exist*.

As a child watching the moon landings in the 1960s, I was struck by one detail during the coverage of Neil Armstrong – ever since childhood his dream had *always* been to walk on the moon. He *never* gave up on it. Neil Armstrong fulfilled his ambition through determination and positive thinking.

Do you know your life purpose? What was your reason for getting up this morning? If you're clear on that, if you've already found whatever makes your heart sing, we're going to improve on that. If you *don't* have a focus that drives your life, this book will help you find it. If your purpose has been foisted upon you by other people, *The Butterfly Experience* will show you how to change that. The techniques I am about to teach you are simple, yet too few people work with them. Why? Because they don't understand their *necessity*.

Each of us is in the process of building our lives, so we need a solid, structured plan to follow. *The Butterfly Experience* is going to provide you with a guide which, if adhered to, promises success. Our experience starts with who we are today and shows us how we can get to where we want to be.

Its ultimate aim is to help us fulfil our destiny. In order to feel fulfilled we need to know what we need to change. We need aims, so we can grow to our full potential. Unless we are connected to the world in some joyous, fulfilling way, we cannot love ourselves as we should. Without self-love, our view of the world is tarnished. But when we learn to love ourselves magic happens, deep inside.

In his Nobel Prize acceptance speech, Dr Martin Luther King said the most important ingredient for success was *self-belief*. We have to feel proud of who we are. Creating your Butterfly Blueprint will give your life *significance*. It will increase your sense of self worth.

By using your Butterfly Blueprint you will set out to do what's necessary, and do it to the best of your ability. This life plan will motivate you and increase your determination. When the door of opportunity opens, it will give you the courage to walk through. It will help you study harder, work harder, create solutions to problems as they occur. It'll help you get out of bad situations instead of hanging on, hoping they'll improve.

Having a plan doesn't mean we're immune from bad experiences, but when things do happen that are out of our control, your Butterfly Blueprint will help you make the right choices. It will hold you accountable. A Butterfly Blueprint helps us realise our strengths and to work on our limitations. It helps us understand that we fail only when we give up.

Be very clear – *The Butterfly Experience* is the key to your life. My life has changed beyond recognition since I developed the techniques in this book. I have used them to change my thinking so that now I live a life without limitations. Life is not a mystery, something to be feared, but a joyous journey.

Mapping out your path isn't difficult, when you have the tools.

Again, the starting point is the same for us all. It's our sub-conscious, our essence. We are what we think. The sub-conscious mind never shuts down. Even when we're sleeping it's busy processing our thoughts. So it stands to reason we should understand it better.

2

A Change In Attitude

The purpose of *The Butterfly Experience* is to get you thinking positively about your life. In the West we're just beginning to understand the value of positive thinking. Schools and businesses know how crucial it is to develop a positive culture. Even in my home country, Scotland, where dourness and negativity are legend, people are becoming increasingly aware of how Positive Thinking – and its opposite force - can shape our lives. Since childhood I have understood that my life, my destiny is controlled by my thoughts. From an early age I've used positive thinking to create the life I deserve.

I have *always* sent wishes out to the universe. This was something innate, untaught, which I've done automatically all my life. Fanatic about sports as a child, I regularly visualised myself running through the tape and being awarded a gold medal. That vision became reality.

My visualisation was so powerful it allowed me to back my wish up with action, always with an end goal in sight. Positive thinking has allowed me to overcome a marriage breakdown, redundancy, the grief of bereavement. It has been the secret behind every success I have ever had – opening a centre for Clinical Hypnosis in Glasgow and training with Positive Thinking leaders from all over the world.

It brought me my beautiful home, fashioned the relationships I have with my amazing husband and children. It is the source of my happiness. We have to get rid of the idea that we are limited in what we can ask for. That belief system has to change. We are conditioned over the years to believe certain things – thoughtless comments by teachers, colleagues and parents form our thinking. But please remember that these limiting beliefs can be changed. You can change them NOW.

Throughout our lives we learn constantly. Experiences and emotions are stored in our minds, just like the data on a computer, though of course the brain is far more powerful. It receives, records and stores information continually. Our brains are divided into two parts, the conscious and the sub-conscious. The conscious is the 'awareness' part of our mind, always thinking, evaluating, wondering what's right or wrong, what's true or untrue.

The *sub-conscious* stores all our memories and experiences, good and bad. Our sub-conscious is programmed to *accept* all information and record it as fact. It doesn't question morality. *The sub-conscious doesn't question. It accepts.* So if information is repeated over and over, our sub-conscious doesn't doubt whether it's true or untrue. It just stores the data as fact.

This is great if we store only positive emotions, but for most of us that's not reality. We all have negative thoughts stored in our sub-conscious since earliest childhood, memories, real or perceived, ideas that have been mulled over and over. If primary carers told us we were stupid, if our teachers told us we were lazy or no good, those ideas were stored in our subconscious - stored in our *belief system*. The messages our brain received became *fact*.

We are programmed from childhood to believe certain things about ourselves. We *learn* behaviours which condition us. We grow the protective shell I spoke about earlier. Here's the good news – *The Butterfly Experience* can help you *unlearn* them. We don't have to keep believing those voices from the past. You *can* break out of your shell.

> *'Beautiful and graceful, varied and enchanting,*
> *small but approachable,*
> *butterflies lead you to the sunny side of life.*
> *And everyone deserves a little sunshine'*
>
> Jeffrey Glassberg

Let Me Tell You About Positive Thinking. Positive Thinking means controlling your thought life, in order to achieve your personal destiny. Positive Thinking means feeling in charge of your life, feeling full of joy. Positive Thinking means creating a wish list and making it happen.

Okay, hands up now. There is probably a wee voice in the back of your head saying, 'It's alright for her, but that psychobabble wouldn't work for me'. With that attitude and negative thinking there's no way you can have an abundant life. You need to change your thinking. *The Butterfly Experience* frees the mind and stops it holding on to negative emotions, behaviours and attitudes.

Make a decision to *START NOW.* Choose to do the things you want. Have the career you want. Be in control of your life. Choose better health, higher energy levels, emotions that feel good. Coming through *The Butterfly Experience* you'll automatically develop a positive mindset. That in turn will attract opportunities. And those changes will ripple out, affecting family, friends and colleagues.

I want to give you a powerful example of how what happens inside our hearts *matters*. When 9/11 happened, people the world over sent America powerful, loving thoughts. I believe that energy healed America. Despite the suffering they endured, the country was fizzing with energy that eased the nation's pain. If a whole country can be helped to heal, what could you achieve in your life? Love is the strongest emotion we have. Love can heal the world. But it has to start with love of *self*. If we all loved ourselves and each other more the energy throughout the entire world would change. There would be no more fighting, no more hunger, no more killing.

The healing can start with us. *The Butterfly Experience* affects how you feel about yourself. It affects how you act, so your whole life improves. Just think of the joy a beautiful butterfly gives to others – and remember how short life is. Think change. Think butterfly.

3

Here's How *The Butterfly Experience* Works

We are beginning to understand how we can use it to heal our bodies. We can *also* heal our spirits. In fact, when the spirit is balanced, the body follows. Through choosing *The Butterfly Experience* you've already begun to think positively. Here's the next step. By understanding how our subconscious influences our thinking for good or bad, we can change our negative self-beliefs for the better. I want to help you understand *the mechanics of your mind* even better. To quote a well-known shampoo ad, now for the science bit…

There are four different states of brain activity: DELTA, BETA, ALPHA and THETA.

I know, you're thinking, 'Sounds like a lot of old Greek to me'. But remember, you wanted to open your mind up to new concepts? Stick with me here… These brain states are all happening within you, right now, whether you are aware of them or not. I want you to learn to maximise them.

DELTA is the slowest brain activity of all four states. The name makes me think of a river, slow moving, broadening out. It's the state of sleep and healing. When we're told to 'sleep on it' this is the wisdom of the ages. DELTA heals our bodies and our minds. In DELTA we are restored. Our mind is fully updated, reorganised. We awake the next morning refreshed and re-energised for what the day will bring.

BETA is the state of alertness and concentration. It is called the waking or logical state. It's a state of heightened alertness. It allows you to think quickly, accessing information stored in the brain. We are in BETA going about our everyday lives. At certain times BETA heightens - your mind becomes more sharply focused. We are in a heightened BETA state, for example, when preparing to take exams. Sportsmen are in this state when performing.

In BETA we have choices to make. A student is asked to give a talk in class. His adrenalin is pumping. 'Fight or Flight', his physiological response to stress, kicks in. He can give the talk and deal with the emotions he's feeling. Or he can run away. You are reading this book in BETA. Thoughts and emotions are coming up in you all the time. For example, you may be frightened of self-relaxation, even though intellectually you understand its benefits. Which are *you* going to choose? Change? Or the status quo? Fight or flight?

ALPHA is the brain state which governs Visualisation and Relaxation. This is the state we need to find ourselves in to <u>maximise the self-relaxation exercises</u> I'm about to teach you.

Brain activity slows down, relaxing us as we move into the ALPHA wave state. Our awareness expands, though we may *feel* half asleep. This is the state which allows us to be creative, to think of new ideas. In ALPHA worries and fears disappear. It is the state of daydreaming. It helps alleviate stress. Paradoxically, though we might seem most vulnerable, this is the strongest state of all. When our brain is in the ALPHA state, it is at its most receptive.

ALPHA is the state in which we access the 'good stuff', the ideas that change our lives - usually while doodling or daydreaming, not trying too hard. FriendsReunited creators Julie and Steve Pankhurst were discussing how to tell friends that Julie was expecting their first child. Julie was in the Alpha state, daydreaming, when the idea for a web site which could bring together old friends was born.

THETA governs Meditation, Memory and Intuition. This is the next state, the one *after* relaxation. Brain activity slows down completely, though not to the point of sleep. This is the state where *the magic happens*. This is where we use our intuition, where we get new ideas and inspiration. In THETA we access all those long forgotten memories and mind pictures. In it we remember dreams, rediscover events we thought long forgotten. In THETA we can recall them easily, learn lessons from them. In THETA we learn to see the past with new eyes.

Sometimes in THETA we feel as though we are floating in our own inner world. This is the state where we can re-programme our minds. In it we can access wonder, see ourselves living an astonishing life. THETA is the state of self-hypnosis. I can't overemphasise the importance of this state – it's the key to evolving, the key to Positive Thinking. It's the Holy Grail. It's the essence of spirituality. It's where we find ourselves and our Higher Self.

THETA is where it all happens – where we make positive changes that revolutionise our lives. Excited? You should be!

Now you have a clearer idea of how your mind works, let's use that information to help de-clutter your thinking. Don't let fear stop you. This stuff is uncomplicated - if you want to be happy then do things that make you happy. If you want to feel happy, think happy thoughts. Mind-blowingly simple.

By now you're starting to really think about your own life. About what needs to change. That's good. But I know you need a little reassurance. Change – even the thought of change – can be very scary. I'm about to give you a precious gift that will help you deal with any fears that arise as you move through *The Butterfly Experience*. I'm going to teach you how to *relax*.

> *'Agenda for today: breathe out, breathe in, and breathe out'*
> The Buddha

Saint Thomas Aquinas believed the world was unhappy because of people's 'inability to sit quietly in a room'. What if all you needed to be happy was to sit quietly? We spend all our time and energy looking for power in externals unaware of the power within ourselves. Just look at the way we discharge negative energy – through addictions, shopping, casual cruelty to others, harmful behaviours, unfulfilling sex. What if you didn't need designer labels or the latest technological gadget to be happy? What if you could find joy just by going inside yourself? If you could connect with your purpose, knowing instinctively the part you need to play in the world?

> *'Faith has to do with things that are not seen,*
> *and hope with things that are not in hand'*
> Saint Thomas Aquinas

Today you are going to learn a tool so vital to your well-being that you will wonder how you ever lived without it. My simple technique for self-relaxation will *change your life*. It is a gift that should be taught to every child in the country. It's called going within.

> *'Happiness is a butterfly, which when pursued*
> *is always just beyond your grasp, but which*
> *if you will sit down quietly, may alight upon you'*
>
> Nathaniel Hawthorne

Lo Tzu, the Chinese philosopher, wrote, 'Muddy water, let stand, becomes clear'. Our thoughts are cluttered by the unimportant. They rob us of energy. Only when your mind is still and empty can you fill it with happy, positive thoughts. The technique I am about to teach you harnesses that ability. It allows you to focus on what really matters.

Self-relaxation or meditation comes from Eastern philosophy, but people from all over the world can benefit from this simple technique. It requires discipline and perseverance – establish it within your daily routine *and* follow it through. Don't give up after a few days. Embedding this spiritual discipline in your life will quickly pay dividends. You don't have to take my word for it. Buddhist monks, renowned for their calm and compassion, spend time going inwards every day.

Through meditation the monks heal themselves physically and mentally. They are probably the most disease-free people on the planet. Instead of fighting life, they go with its flow. Buddhists – even those who are cloistered – still have to contend with life's daily frustrations.

Through meditation they learn to have control over their reactions. They learn to *choose* joy. They don't fear challenges. Instead they look for the lessons to be learned. They *expect* to grow through their experiences. This is self-relaxation at its best – a daily, conscious decision to focus on the positive.

One of the great teachings of Buddhism is recognising that we cause much of our stress ourselves, through our expectations of ourselves and others. When we feel down, depressed, angry or simply feel things are going wrong, we are usually *out of touch* with ourselves.

34

What if you could change your life by just being in the moment? What if that 'quiet time' made you a different person, with different values and a very different quality of life? It's time to take back control. It's time to avoid burn out, exhaustion and long-term illness. The next few pages will teach you how to *relax*, to go inside yourself to discover the *treasure within.*

Self-relaxation is a perfectly natural state, just like daydreaming. It's our richest source of ideas and inspiration. You don't need a guru or life coach or hypnotherapist to find it. You have the power to access it right now. Combine it with the visualisation I'll teach you later and you have a powerful force for good.

I can almost hear you saying 'Meditation? Tried that. Didn't work!' I can hear others groaning, saying they don't have enough time as it is. How much time do you spend glued to garbage on the TV or poring over celebrity magazines?

Everyone can find fifteen minutes a day to radically improve their lives. You have the choice right now. It's been said that the beginning of wisdom is the willingness to look at things in a different way. Throw off the negative thinking that's telling you, 'This will never work' or 'I feel foolish'. Your inner child is ready. DO IT TODAY, otherwise tomorrow will just be a repeat of your current experience.

The only thought you need to have right now is, *change*. Understand that what you have been doing up till now hasn't been enough for you. You need new thinking. New ideas. New practices.

Forget everything you think you know about self-relaxation and meditation. Accept that there is no right or wrong way to do things. The way you choose to proceed is the right way for you. I've seen people spend hundreds of pounds and untold hours in stress management courses, coming away more frustrated than ever. This is different. This is the start of the beginning of a new positive routine. Again I want to emphasise, you will feel the difference *immediately.* You will become calm, relaxed and more focused in your thought processes.

Self-relaxation and self-hypnosis are the same. Both terms describe a light trance, an altered state of the mind. The purpose of self-relaxation is to make our minds calm and peaceful. It is the most important thing we can do to help ourselves. Self-relaxation will

35

actually slow your heart rate. It will make your thinking more focused and alert. It will energise you. Instead of waiting for happy times, we can create them using this technique. Everyone can do it – in fact we do it automatically.

I'm asking you to lay aside all prejudgements – that's just another word for prejudice! Just go with the directions on the next few pages. They will *change* your life.

Read through this exercise and then you are ready to practice. Be prepared to amaze yourself. Everything starts with a conscious decision. Learning self-relaxation marks the beginning of a new chapter in your life. Commit to taking ten to fifteen minutes each day, preferably in the morning.

Be disciplined. Think of it like a deep-sea diver checking his air supply. Allow nothing to divert you from this quiet time. It will dictate the quality of your day.

Find a quiet place. Choose your favourite chair and sit with a straight back in order to align your spine and allow your feet to rest on the floor. Make yourself comfortable. Remove your glasses if you wear them.

You will soon come to feel your own energy and feel very at peace. This feeling will grow each time you do your self-relaxation. If for any reason you have to awaken during the relaxation, you can do so by simply opening your eyes. You will be fully wide-awake. You can return to your self-relaxation at a later time.

Before you begin, decide on three affirmations, positive statements in the present tense that you will include in your relaxation. For example: 'I am a confident person', 'I approve of myself', 'I am healthy and happy'.

Now - allow yourself to relax. Feel your body supported by the chair. In your own time, allow your eyes to comfortably CLOSE. Become aware of your breathing. Breathing in and on your out breath begin to slowly and mentally start counting at *ten*, breathing in and on the out breath mentally count *nine*, and then continue counting down to *one* on each out breath. With each descending number, on your out breath, you will become more relaxed - ten per cent more relaxed. Breathing freely and easily.

Staying deeply relaxed, you will soon find that your mind begins to wander, maybe to a favourite place. Your mind will choose the right place for you, no need to fight the thought. It may be a beach, a garden, or a favourite room.

You aren't bound to it – from time to time the place you use, your sanctuary, may change. There is no need to fight it now. Your mind will automatically wander to the safest place, where you are secure, where no one can harm you.

Imagine a white light shining down from above and allow it to melt down through your head, your crown chakra, down to the tip of your toes, giving you calmness, peace and contentment.

Spend time there. Relax, unwind. Feel the white light re-energise your body and allow your body to refocus.

You may experience a floating sensation. Don't worry. It's simply a sign that your body is relaxing.

You may experience a sensation of warmth, perceive smells, and even see colours.

Spend time there, giving yourself positive affirmations, making positive statements about yourself, to yourself. Choose one thing you want to concentrate on, make it realistic, e.g. a healthier you.

NOW imagine yourself - the way you want to be. See yourself content, smiling, healthier. If you have a problem, see it fixed. See yourself living the life you want. The job you want, the house, the holidays, the family and feel as if you are already that person living that life. Feel what it feels like; allow the energy to enter every muscle and cell in your body.

You can go to this place at any time, on any day you choose. This is your space, your special place. To awaken yourself, count from one to ten. At the count of *eight*, open your eyes. Tell yourself you feel refreshed, re-energised, and more confident. You feel more in control. You have a greater sense of well-being.

FEEL HOW GOOD THAT WAS!

(Using The Butterfly Experience - Transforming Lives Self Relaxation CD available separately can enhance each of the Relaxations in this book.)

Take those precious ten to fifteen minutes a day and watch your life change. It changes you at a fundamental, cellular level. It will change at a psychological level - as soon as you begin to use self-relaxation to improve your mindset, you'll wonder why you never did it before. You'll find space in your head to look at where you are going and even begin to see possibilities of how to get there. And it will change you at a spiritual level.

Self-relaxation is the most therapeutic tool you can learn. It calms your mind, controls your emotions.

We're not responsible for the thoughts we have, but we are responsible for how long we hold on to them.

When we learn to train our minds it becomes so easy to replace our negative thoughts with positive ones. We become more balanced. Acquiring this skill can bring new emotions to the surface. It helps us to understand ourselves. No more hiding from the truth of our emotions.

We feel happy, content, relaxed, fulfilled. Success with this technique breeds success in life. People who use it gain acceptance of themselves and others. They see clearly what they need to do to move on in their lives. They make positive changes and transform their lives for the better. They choose to be happy. They choose to deal with problems instead of allowing themselves to become overwhelmed.

Start living your new life today. It only takes a little courage and a little faith.

4

Butterfly Affirmations

We've spoken about the subconscious and its role in our happiness. By using Butterfly Affirmations we can train our mind to be more positive. Butterfly Affirmations are basically positive statements that we say over and over to ourselves until we start to believe them.

Butterfly Affirmations will change your belief system. Change your habitual thinking and you change your life for the better. If you believe that you don't deserve to stay in a beautiful home, chances are you don't like where you're living presently. It's no one's fault you have that belief. But it's your responsibility to do something about it. Whenever I begin work with my patients I ask them to use positive affirmations.

It's vital that we start off the day the right way, by programming our subconscious. Affirmations are very powerful, positive statements said in the present tense. They are especially wonderful when we're low or need a pick-me-up. I tell my patients to repeat them to themselves three times on awakening, for example, 'I am feeling confident', 'I am feeling happy' or 'I am calm and full of energy'.

The Butterfly Experience asks us to choose three positive affirmations to say each day. Here are a few to start you off:-

- I am open and willing to change
- I love myself exactly as I am
- I am filled with abundance
- Energy is flowing through my body

Say your Butterfly Affirmations with feeling and emotion. Really mean them. As you say them you may not be feeling happy. Remember we can 'trick' the subconscious - if you say it, your subconscious will believe it. Before you know it you will be behaving like a happy person. Your attitude will change. You will act and feel as if you are that person you've visualised, confident and healthy.

It is important to note that you should write down your Butterfly Affirmations as this reinforces the message in your mind. Remember you are working only on your self-belief system and vibrational energy. Others need to do this work for themselves. When meditating, you can ask in general terms for help for others, but focus on your own needs and desires.

I know for some of you this may feel strange, outlandish even. But look at it this way – what you've been doing up till now hasn't been working properly; otherwise you wouldn't be reading this book. If you take the steps *The Butterfly Experience* teaches and apply my techniques then you too can live your dream. Each of us is searching for that elusive 'something', the missing piece of the jigsaw that when it clicks into place will make all our wishes come true. That 'something' lies deep inside you right now. You can be happy, healthy, confident, positive and abundantly rich, starting right now – just trust the process. By using Butterfly Affirmations you will start to change the habitual patterns of your mind. Affirmations change the negative beliefs that you hold deep within your sub-conscious.

Our mindset is paramount.

HAVE YOU SAID YOUR BUTTERFLY AFFIRMATIONS FOR TODAY?

Turn to your *Butterfly Journal* at the back of the book and write your three Butterfly Affirmations for today. Say them three times each both morning and night, every day. Say them with feeling. Believe them. For example, 'I have a wonderful new job and am filled with happiness'. You may still be looking for the perfect job, but by saying your Butterfly Affirmation you'll have more energy to find it.

Now that you're in a more positive frame of mind, it's time to really focus on your life. What follows now are more written exercises. For your Butterfly Blueprint you need to establish where you are, right this moment. Remember, it doesn't matter what anyone else thinks here.

We're looking for the steps *you* need to take to be happier.

Exercise One

What does happiness mean to you? How many of us have actually asked ourselves that question? Take a few minutes to think about it!

Turn to the *Butterfly Journal* and write down a list of things that make you happy, e.g. spending time with your friends, going to the cinema, your favourite foods. Write down the things you like to do. Think about the little things in life that make you content. When you were a child, playing on a swing, feeling the air rush by – that feeling of freedom was *enough*.

No cares or worries…what does that for you today? Relaxing in a bath? Painting your nails? Playing a game of golf? Reading a good book? What makes you happy and content? What makes you fizz with joy? Write it down – list them, make them real.

Exercise Two

Now take a moment to think of what you want to *change* to better your life. Write them down – all those things you've never really admitted to anyone else. Seven is a magical number, so *The Butterfly Experience* asks you to write seven things in your life that need changing. Remember, the butterfly goes through a constant process of changing and discarding in order to take flight.

Don't be frightened – this list is just for you. You are in control. Just seven honest admissions, for example weight issues, debt, friends who make you feel vulnerable, loneliness, your job prospects. Notice how your body reacts as you say them out loud. Feel your body tightening in fear and anger.

This is your body's gift, telling you not to accept these things any more. Your body is telling you to make some serious decisions. I need you to think now about every area of your life – job satisfaction, relationships, leisure time, ambitions, etc. Ask yourself to be really honest, giving each part of your life a mark out of ten. Where do you feel you're in a rut? Are you happy at work? Do you enjoy the friends

41

you have? What about your relationships – are they working? Do they sustain you? Face up to the truth of your life. Be ruthlessly honest. What do you have to lose? Think about it, things can't get any worse.

Change begins with a thought. You've just agreed certain aspects of your life are making you miserable. Step out of your comfort zone. It's not as scary as you think - you may even like it. By writing down your honest thoughts about your life you have taken power away from the negative and given it to the positive. You know now what's not working and what needs to change. You have greater honesty and self-awareness.

Now that you have admitted that you want to change, let's get started doing just that. How? By becoming open to new ideas.

Let's go back to that list. Decide what things in your life make you feel negative and decide to get rid of them *today*. Identify and weed out the friends who are pulling you down. Decide to stop doing the things that make you unhappy. If you're being taken advantage of, make a conscious decision to find a way of sharing the load with others. This is your life – it's too precious to waste.

Exercise Three

Now I want you to think of all the good things you have in your life. It's an old fashioned idea I'm hoping to teach the world again. It's called counting our blessings. We're too caught up in the material world. We think if we have a bigger house, a faster car, if we win the lottery, then we'll be happy. Well, I have news for you. Happiness cannot be bought. You get it for free.

What do you have to be grateful for? Right here, right now? Health, a home, a loving family, a career, food on the table? These are the things that should make us happy. So write down the things that your life has been blessed with – a gratitude list.

Now write down all the things you're good at. This is no time for false modesty. You're building your future happiness.

Now that you know how to count your blessings, you've made a start in thinking in a more positive manner. Now that you know you have so many things to be grateful for, start acting that way. Stop judging others. Be kind. Smile. Make a commitment to give yourself a regular pat on the back.

You're growing, learning. See what the universe has given you already? Why would it not give you more?

Exercise Four

Change is already happening. Gifts have begun 'flying at you through the darkness'. The larva is starting to gnaw its way out of the shell.

Time for a new list. Start thinking about what you really want from life. Think about the butterfly, its beautiful, vibrant colours. What would make you take flight? Using your journal write down: 'I am willing to be open to change'. Sign it and date your signature. Now write: 'I desire' and start writing your wish list.

A list by definition includes more than one item. This is no time to be shy. This is your life; believe the universe will provide all that you want. Remember – it's all waiting inside you. Look into your heart. Really search your heart's true desires.

Write them down in the present tense, as though they were already in your life, e.g. I love my new car with its four doors and leather seats. I am very happy in my new relationship. I am financially secure.

What makes you feel excited when you think about it? What dreams did you have as a child that you've let go of? Where would you go tomorrow if money were no object? What would you do?

Add the dreams you'd be too embarrassed to admit even to your best friend – the more outlandish the better. Don't ask for money - it never comes in the form of cash. You may be looking for a new home and find yourself with a new job or a promotion to finance it. It's what you would do with the money if you had it that's important. Think really hard. What do you really want? No matter how far off they seem today, get those dreams down on paper. Something magical happens when we write things down. They acquire power. Soon you're going to start to make these dreams grow. I'm going to show you how to nurture them. You'll soon see that they're not so remote after all.

Now for the big one...write down the things that, if you were asked on your deathbed, you would be sorry not to have done.

Congratulations on completing the first exercises of your Butterfly Blueprint! You know what you have to be grateful for. You know what's working for you and what's not. You know *what you want*.

It's time to accept the rewards that life has for you. It's time to take the next step.

Remember, this is an inside job. If we are to create the life we deserve we need a starting place. Your character, your unique set of abilities are that place. It's time to take stock of what you have and what you'll need.

Exercise Five

Give me a list now of all the good qualities you possess. If you get stuck, ask a parent or a friend. Go deep. Any compliment you've ever been given, write it down. Remember, we need this to be as positive as possible, so we don't skimp here out of false pride. Be honest.

When a butterfly lays its eggs they're held firmly in place by a special substance, almost glue-like, that keeps the new life safe and allows it to grow. So what's the glue that will hold your new life together? I'm talking about self-belief and confidence.

Confidence isn't as elusive as you think. To be a confident person all we have to do is accept ourselves for who we are. Each of us is a one-off, a combination of unique gifts and talents. Using the same Butterfly Affirmation technique as above, I want you to use the material you've just written to create affirmations you believe about yourself. You've just established what they are, e.g. 'I am confident and happy'. 'I am creative and trustworthy'. 'I am a confident person'.

Look back over them. Thank yourself for them. Each gift is needed if we are to achieve our full potential and help others to grow. Claim them as yours.

Exercise Six

People who are confident believe in their own abilities. Self-belief attracts more opportunities. Being open to what life has to offer makes them feel stronger, so they become more confident. The key is believing you are worthy.

I want you to sieve your way through your own thoughts about yourself. Again, we're going to choose seven positive thoughts. Straight away pick out any negatives. Now that you recognise the negative thoughts about yourself, it's possible to recognise them if they appear in the future. Put them to the side for the moment. Finish your list of seven positive qualities.

You can start to see the real you emerging. Recognise that your natural character and abilities are your precious gift. *The Butterfly Experience* is going to help you develop them, rather than wishing for the impossible. If you stay in your natural character you can achieve anything. No matter what happens, or who tries to put you down, if you believe in yourself your life will change.

Exercise Seven

Now go back to your journal, to the categories of your life you really want to change, e.g. career, family, relationships and finance. It's time to focus on these areas.

Write Butterfly Affirmations for each category. Career – 'I am a hard worker properly rewarded for my efforts'. Home – 'I am happily married with a wonderful family'. Social Life – 'I have great friends'. Finance – 'I am able to pay my bills easily'. Spiritually – 'I am aligned with Spirit'.

Now that you've written them, I want you to use them. These are your personal mantras.

As we come to the end of this first stage on your journey, here are seven tasks I want you to begin building into your day.

TASK ONE

From now on refer regularly to your list of good points. Add to it as new thoughts occur to you.

Write down compliments you receive, good things that people have said about you. Now look at the list of things you want to be rid of or improve. It could be your self-image. It might be your weight. It could be you want to create better relationships. You decide. Start working on these areas.

Your awareness of them has been raised. Look for opportunities to bring positive experiences into these areas of your life. Remember to use your self-relaxation and Butterfly Affirmations to help you.

TASK TWO

'Fake it until you make it'. If you act confidently then others will treat you differently. We teach others how to treat us by our attitude and our body language. The following chapter will teach you more about these vital skills. For now stand tall, look people in the eye and smile!

TASK THREE

Surround yourself with positive, confident people. Model aspects of them. Seek them out. Your own confidence will grow as a result. My mother is always positive. Through her I learned the value of Positive Thinking. I admire her so much for her strength of character. The positive lessons she taught me as a child have stayed with me all my life. My whole childhood rang with phrases like 'Keep going, even when times are hard.' 'Never give up!' and 'Your reward is waiting just over the hill'.

TASK FOUR

We are all under constant pressure to be the perfect shape, to be glamorous, rich and successful, have perfect teeth and perfect families. Yet if we look around, how many of us approach that ideal? See yourself as a valuable human being instead of feeling shy, weak or insecure. Accept who you are today – remember this is just the beginning. Decide to give yourself a break. Acknowledge you've been doing the best you could and that you're changing. Your attitude about yourself will change very quickly too.

TASK FIVE

Go to different places, look to make new friends. Practice acting more confidently. Remember everyone is feeling as nervous as you are.

You don't need a title to be important. All you need to be happy is already within yourself. Grab opportunities with both hands. We all face challenges in life. Jumping over our own shyness and inhibitions is vital. Ask others questions about themselves. Show an interest in them, instead of worrying about the impression you're making. A small change in perspective, but it can bring huge dividends.

TASK SIX

Stop taking your life for granted. LIVE EVERY DAY AS IF IT WERE YOUR LAST! Ask yourself what you could do today that would make you feel happy and proud. Take a step towards it. To be esteemed you have to do estimable acts. And nothing gives us a healthier sense of self than helping others. Think of something you could do to make a difference in someone else's life. And don't take credit for it!

TASK SEVEN

Choose the positive. Every day of our lives gives us added knowledge that takes us further on our journey. What have you learned to date? Do you still hold grudges about family, friends or colleagues? Are you still bitter about some unresolved conflict? Let it go now. It's time. All it takes is the realisation that you're hurting yourself time and time again by reliving the initial hurt.

This foundation stage provides the butterfly with everything it needs to move beyond its protective shell and on to the next stage of growth. Before we finish this stage, I want to talk now about a vital element of your life you may have been overlooking in your search for growth. Again, it's in the last place you would have thought to look – inside yourself. It's one of our most precious gifts and it's called... *Trusting Our Instincts.*

5

Trusting Our Instincts

The Butterfly Experience demands that we learn this skill. Every human being has this sixth sense – we know it as a 'gut feeling', that inner feeling that tells us what's right. Our gift of intuition or inner wisdom is so precious yet we constantly ignore it. Children use their intuition all the time; they are so open and intuitive. But as they grow older they face pressure and begin to turn from it. Advances in science and technology have benefited society greatly, but intangibles like our intuition have been neglected. We've forgotten how to trust this great gift.

Our ability to connect with our Higher Self has been lost. It's our built-in safety mechanism. It's the voice of Spirit who wants the very best for us. But here's the good news. The more we use our intuition the more it develops. Sonia Choquette, author of *Trust Your Vibes*, talks of human beings in terms of five and six sensory people. I call myself a sixth sensory person, because I've listened to my intuition all my life, knowing that if something doesn't feel right I should walk away.

How often have you intuitively feared something and dismissed that fear? That feeling you ignored was your body's ancient wisdom. Sonia confronts five sensory people about 'sitting on the fence'. We sometimes use phrases like, 'I had a weird feeling' or 'I had this odd sensation'. Why not just come out and say it was your intuition? There are dozens of phrases in our vernacular – 'sleep on it' or 'if in doubt leave it out' - that bear this idea out.

Can you imagine the consequences of relying on this inner knowing? Can you imagine using it in your daily life – listening to people, intuitively knowing the right thing to do or say? Our intuition is also known as our 'third eye'. It is a centre of knowingness some believe is located between our eyebrows. When you connect with it, it is as though your life is switched on. No one can teach you this skill – you have to feel for it yourself. You'll know when you find it. Tap back into that intuition.

Build on the butterfly techniques I'm teaching you. Practice them daily. With just a little persistence you will see changes almost immediately.

You can't understand how powerful these techniques are unless you try them. You need to reject negative thinking at a cellular level. We need to be ruthless, accepting only the best of ourselves. To do that, we need to learn discernment. We need to understand what strengthens us and what weakens us. So if you've just been reading these pages and not *doing* the work, go back now and do it now. A few hours to change your entire life? How can you *not* do it?

Only move on to the next stage when you've completed the work in this section, when you understand who you are and why you think the way you do. Move forward only when you've admitted what's stopping you achieving your goals. Give yourself permission to become whole. Wipe the slate clean and start again.

You only have to become willing to change and then the universe will help you. You don't need to worry about how or when. It will happen in universal time. If you start today then you are one day closer to that dream.

When you've done the work in this section I want you to cement your commitment to this process. Not a half-hearted, I-kind-of-get-what-she's-talking-about piecrust promise. I'm talking about a firm contract with yourself, to act and think more positively in life. In *all* areas of your life. It's time to draw that line in the sand. *Make the choice today* to make the best of *The Butterfly Experience*, to think in a healthier way, to change your life.

MAKE A COMMITMENT TO YOURSELF HERE AND NOW!
Contract

I agree today to be willing to be open to change

Signed: ....…..…. Date: ....

GROWING PAINS

6

Caterpillar Section

The Caterpillar stage helps us look at our lives and decide what to keep and what to jettison. Caterpillars grow at a phenomenal rate. You should expect rapid growth in this cycle too.

Change seems scary – in fact we avoid it like the plague. But when we resist 'change' we flow against universal energy. We tighten our muscles, we bring on disease. By now you've grown strong enough to survive outside the protective walls you had created. Remember, things change all the time, things we welcome. New job, new car, new friends, new experiences. Change means making choices, taking action. Think about all the positive changes you've experienced: first love, learning a new skill, discovering a new talent.

Though the thought of change seems scary, remember the alternative. You can stay a caterpillar forever. Never be a butterfly. It's your choice. What I'm offering you in this section is personal freedom – no more, no less. It's time to expand and grow. It's time to shed the negative.

Just as butterflies are different from species to species, caterpillars differ too. Some are dull, easily overlooked. Some are good at hiding. Some manage to camouflage themselves better than others. Some caterpillars go quietly about their business. Others have bright stripes which warn others to keep back. Some have bristles or spikes, and can seem downright menacing. Which caterpillar are you? And what do you need to shed in order to grow? It's time to talk about...*Owning Our Emotions*.

7

Owning Our Emotions

We cannot fully know the joys of life without having experienced first the darker side. We all have painful events in our lives. It's a common reaction for people to shrug off past hurts. Some of our hurts are so deeply buried, that we manage to convince ourselves that we're over them. But unless you deal with them, that's what you're giving your subconscious to work with. By doing your self-relaxation you can learn to forgive, to 'let go' and start to heal your life.

No one is denying that bad stuff happens. How do you react to it *today*? If thinking about past hurts is still hurting you, you need to find a way to move past them. What's stored in your subconscious that's causing you pain? In *The Butterfly Experience* we think of thoughts and emotions as the building blocks for our new life.

We are so conscious nowadays of what we need to eat to stay healthy. What we need to realise is that it's just as important that we feed our minds in order to stay well. It is so important to feed our mind positive language. Think about your self-talk. How often do you tell yourself, 'I feel awful, I really don't feel good'? What do you think your mind does with that negative information? It acts accordingly. Even if you tell yourself you don't have a headache, your mind still hears the word 'headache'.

Deprived of spiritual nourishment, our minds struggle. Most of us spend more time on our cars. We buy senseless stuff for our homes. We waste money on clothes in order to impress others. We burden ourselves with debt, all for the sake of what other people think. The Caterpillar stage will allow you to look at these things and evaluate them for what they are. Watch your thoughts.

'Our thoughts create our lives'

Louise L Hay

The Butterfly Experience will ask you to consider your thought processes. How and what we think determines our future. So let's make sure that the material we're working with is sound. We need to reject any thinking that's inferior, or faulty. The quality of our life depends on it. If we don't check our thinking for faults, this new life we're constructing won't be sound.

Grudging acceptance of this idea won't bring about the changes you need in your life. Remember how strongly the subconscious holds on to ideas. Here's a powerful example.

Out on the town, drinking heavily, a young man became embroiled in an incident. Another man had been stabbed and he was being held responsible. He had suffered a blackout. Desperate, he approached a clinical hypnotherapist. Could he help him recall the events of that evening? After his session, the young man was fully able to recall the incident *and* his role in it. That's the power of the subconscious. *It holds on to those things that the conscious brain forgets.*

That's where *The Butterfly Experience* comes into its own. It positively influences this part of our psyche. With it we learn to accept and let go of negative feelings, the things that threaten our happiness and our equilibrium. It helps us find and enjoy balance in our life.

Over the years I have seen so much disease that could have been avoided if people had only understood the damage they were doing by holding on to anger and ill feeling. Store up enough rancour over a lifetime and you're guaranteeing yourself disease.

Choose the positive. In any given situation *The Butterfly Experience* tells us to choose joy, choose growth. As the caterpillar hatches, it begins to eat – it nourishes itself with good things. I want you to choose only what nourishes you. As the caterpillar devours all the bounty nature offers, it grows.

Gradually its exoskeleton becomes too tight for comfort, so it sheds its skin, revealing new growth underneath. These sheddings go by a wonderful name – 'instars'. The word makes me think of all the potential within us. After each instar, each transformation, the caterpillar is different. It can change dramatically, in colour and appearance, from the instar before.

8

Negative Thoughts Grow With Attention

Henry Ford once said, 'A clean engine always delivers power'. As soon as we realise we are responsible for our own happiness and unhappiness, we can begin to take control of our thoughts and attitudes.

But the reverse is also true. If you allow small negative thoughts to grow then they will soon become mighty negative thoughts. When our mood swings, everything just seems to fall apart. Controlling our thinking also means honouring our emotions. Be honest. What pain has had you reaching for that biscuit barrel recently? What did your spouse say that made you shout at the kids? What were you thinking just before you cut up that driver? Our days are full of thoughts which trigger negative behaviour.

So what can we do about it? We need to be ruthless about the building blocks of thoughts that we have. The Caterpillar stage asks that you:

<u>Learn to forgive yourself</u>. We all make mistakes. 'To err is human' is an ancient spiritual axiom. But too many of us seem unable to forgive ourselves. We all know some people who can't let go of the past. Their life seems full of remorse and bitterness. Those negative emotions metamorphose into depression. I see this so often in my patients. It doesn't have to be that way. Saying we were wrong requires a little humility. But we can only move forward if we look at our past and acknowledge the role we had to play in it.

<u>Learn to forgive others</u>. After an argument or disagreement, even if things are 'reconciled', we can hold on to a residue of anger. Honest communication and a 'win-win' attitude to solving problems will take you a long way.

<u>Learn your own lessons</u>. Perhaps you've learned negative behaviour

and habits from parents or friends. You've watched them hold on to anxieties. Or you're full of anger on their behalf. Remember – this is their lesson. If you diminish it in any way, if you enable them, they will just have to learn the lesson again.

Learn to let go. Ironically, whilst we're holding on to anger, the people we are angry at are carrying on with their own lives. Holding on to the past long term can destroy your happiness. How many of us actually take responsibility for our lives? It's easy to blame others for our problems. It's time to stop pointing the finger and use that energy in a positive way.

Learn to stand up for what you need. Decide your own priorities. For a long time I had wanted to end my first marriage. I didn't leave for fear of hurting my parents. For seven years I stayed, trying ways to make it work, becoming more and more miserable. Finally I made the decision, but I dreaded telling my mum and dad. I'll never forget my mother's words, 'Sit down and I'll get us a cup of tea.' If I had known she would accept my decision so well, I would have left years before. Instead I wasted years *thinking,* allowing my thoughts to run away with themselves and become my truth. My truth was wrong.

Learn to say *sorry.* In my experience the people who struggle with forgiveness find it very hard to forgive themselves. They regard saying 'sorry' as a failure. In fact it is the kindest thing they can do, for themselves and others. If we could learn to forgive without waiting for the other person to come to us first, the world would be changed overnight. If we take the first step, the other person almost always takes the second. Grudges are the main culprits in negative thinking. They limit us, make us live shorter lives. Is it worth dying because you can't forgive?

Learn to let others be themselves. We can't change people – or the past. We can change our attitudes to them. Are you willing to sell your peace of mind for the sake of being vindicated?

You *know* you're right, so let it go! Are you holding on to negative experiences? Sometimes we nurture ill-feeling, because it makes us feel vindicated. It allows us to continue seeing others in a negative way so that we don't have to look at our own behaviour. Had a row with a friend? Instead of walking away, ask yourself why the person

56

is acting that way.

A little hug could be all it takes to turn the situation around. When we're hurting we lash out – why not let go of the hurt and let the healing start with you?

So many people get into the mindset that everything always has to be 'perfect'. What *is* perfect? From where I'm standing everything in life always turns out exactly the way it should – whether that outcome is thought to be good or bad at the time. Everything in the universe is interconnected. It's not a case of bad things happening to good people. The universe gives us opportunities to learn and grow. Change what you can, if you can. If you can't change it, why get upset about it?

> *'God, grant me the Serenity to accept the things I cannot change*
> *Courage to accept the things I can, and the*
> *Wisdom to know the difference'*
>
> Reinhold Niebuhr

We have to learn to let go. All it takes is a decision. The only way of putting negative experiences behind us is to learn from them. No one escapes pain of one kind or another. Whatever the pain, time is the healer. But we can learn to process the experience by learning from it. Buddhists believe that is our real purpose for being here – to learn the lessons we still need to learn. They know that acceptance is the key. Everything that happens is designed to teach us. There *is* no failure if we learn from every experience, ensuring that we never repeat our mistakes. At this vital Caterpillar stage it's vital that we develop the habit of using these experiences, searching them for the pearl of wisdom to be gained from them. But ultimately we have to let the pain go.

Ralph Waldo Emerson understood this.

'Finish each day and be done with it. You have done what you could. Some blunders and absurdities no doubt crept in; forget them as soon as you can. Tomorrow is a new day; begin it well and serenely and with too high a spirit to be cumbered with your old nonsense.'

Butterflies, in order to fly, cannot be burdened. Facing up to our own negative thinking isn't easy – because with it comes the realisation that we've been causing ourselves harm. But the good news is that it stops as of now. Because to become a happier person, you must first *believe* that it's possible.

That comes by knowing we're as happy in any given day as we make up our minds to be. Look at toddlers – sad one minute and the next their tears have dried and they're getting on with the business of living. We need to learn to let go the way our children do.

The more attention we give negative emotions, the worse we are going to feel. The more negative the thought, the bigger it seems. We sink into a morass of negative thoughts. And the vicious cycle starts all over again.

If you have a serious decision to make it's more important than ever to wait until your mood improves. When you are in a higher vibration your head will be clearer and more focused.

'Be the change you want to see in the world'
Mahatma Gandhi

Remember to practice your self-relaxation throughout this stage of the experience. You're learning to fly, remember? This is how we lighten our being, so we can take flight. If you're thinking 'It's too late for me', remember you're never too old to let go of emotional baggage.

Linda came to see me because she couldn't swim. As we began to explore her feelings, she told me she was afraid to let go of the side of the pool. Going deeper, it was clear there was something else Linda didn't want to let go of - the anger she felt towards her father. He had never praised her, despite her many accomplishments. The message she received was that she wasn't good enough. That thought resurfaced in anger and resentment. Using self-relaxation, Linda learned to accept her father. She began to understand he was only doing his best. She learned her thoughts about him were holding her back in every area of her life. She learned to forgive.

I don't want *you* to waste years of your life. Time is a great healer. But we can help it along.

MAKE A CONSCIOUS DECISION TODAY, NO MATTER WHAT'S GOING ON IN YOUR LIFE, TO LEAVE THE PAST

BEHIND AND MOVE ON. CHERISH ALL THE WONDERFUL MOMENTS YOU'VE KNOWN. THANK THE UNIVERSE FOR THE BAD, FOR THE LESSONS THEY HAVE TAUGHT YOU. START TODAY.

It's a universal law that any negative energy we send out comes straight back. It's the boomerang effect. Like attracts like. To break free from unhappiness, you have to bring yourself fully into the present. You must accept that the past is just that - it's passed. Deciding to let go is the hard part. Once that decision is made, life becomes easier. Find someone you can share negative experiences with, someone you can trust. Imagine your life without those negative feelings. What would that feel like?

What sort of a person would you be without those negative feelings weighing you down? Shed what's stopping you grow!

9

RED-X Technique

Here's a fabulous butterfly technique to help you do that. It's the most vital tool in the Caterpillar cycle. I call it my *RED-X Technique.*

The bottom line is that we make our own choices. We choose our actions, our emotions. So we have to learn to control them. Our emotions are rooted in our thought life. Our minds cannot be empty for more than a few seconds; they automatically fill up with thoughts. But those thoughts can be either positive or negative. Do you dwell on your negative thoughts? Or do you want to learn to dismiss them?

This is no mumbo-jumbo. Learning to rid yourself of negative thinking is the best gift you can give yourself. It's life-altering, mind-blowing in its simplicity and possible for any one, under any circumstance. It's free, and it's phenomenal. And it's based on a simple principle.

Here it is: *We can control our thoughts.*

We have over 60,000 thoughts each day, most of them being leftovers from the day before. If they stay in your head they have to be fed and nurtured. Some are good, others negative. We need to acknowledge our negative thoughts, but not allow the body to hold on to them. I'm about to teach you a vital technique. If you adopt it and really apply it in your lives, things will change radically, and very quickly.

Let's imagine it's the day of your driving test. You awake and your first thought is, 'I'll never pass', or 'I'll probably get a tough examiner. I just know I'll fail.' You haven't even got out of bed yet and already your day is a disaster! Let's change those thoughts.

First of all, pick up on the signals your body is giving you - headache, tension, sweaty palms, cramps in your tummy, restlessness. Recognise what you're doing to your body.

Then STOP THE THOUGHT!!! RED-X the negative thought from

your mind. Literally imagine a huge RED-X over it.

Now turn it over – repeat the thought in a positive way. Talk to yourself as if the test has already happened. Remember the subconscious mind doesn't know the difference between true and untrue. 'Fantastic! I passed my driving test!'

Now go into Alpha state. Daydream. Rehearse the day ahead, paint a picture of yourself doing your driving test in a positive and controlled manner. See it in detail, the traffic, the manoeuvres, watch yourself dealing with them, driving effortlessly and easily. Every time a negative thought tries to raise its ugly head, immediately RED-X it from your mind. See yourself passing, being congratulated by the examiner. Feel the pressure of his handshake. Believe you will pass. Very quickly your mind will get the message. Your *attitude* to the impending test will be entirely different. Your body language will be different. Your positive thoughts will reward you with a feeling of calm and composure. And you'll pass the test!

Apply the RED–X technique to all your negative thinking. Get into the habit of monitoring your thinking. You know how badly negative thoughts hurt us. So don't let them through! As soon as you catch yourself thinking negatively, RED-X that thought. Bad habits – and that's all negative thinking is! - take around twenty one days to be broken. Through time you will start to think in a more positive way. A little perseverance and you'll start to feel better, more relaxed and more open. Then just watch the opportunities come your way.

'I hope my meeting goes well today'. A standard thought. But you're subconscious, which has been disappointed in the past, hears only doubt. There's a chance you won't pull this off. Your body language starts signalling that doubt at the meeting, displaying your lack of confidence. Instead, RED-X the thought, then say, 'My meeting went well today', as if it had already happened. The subconscious mind doesn't know if that's true or untrue. When you arrive for the meeting your body already thinks you're a success and you look and feel confident, happy and positive. Your outcome to the meeting is very different.

You replace our thoughts all the time. Imagine you were watching a film at the cinema. Suddenly you think about painting your bedroom blue. Chances are you can simply dismiss the thought with no effort at all. The thought drifts away and you can bring your full attention back to the film. The difference here is that we do it *consciously*. With time, dismissing our negative thoughts using the RED-X method becomes just as natural a process.

Think of it as learning to drive. When we start learning everything seems so difficult and complicated. But in no time you've learned to drive automatically, the slightest pressure on the wheel keeps you on your chosen path. That's how quickly we can learn to dispel negative thinking once we start to see the benefits.

We can use the RED-X technique to stop ourselves being sabotaged by the past too. How often have you walked away from a situation feeling aggrieved, the injured party? What might the outcome have been with a little courage, if you had RED-X'd your fear and asked the questions you had wanted to ask. Or if you had used the RED-X technique to allow yourself to see past negative thoughts to see the situation as it really was?

What thoughts about your past have held you back? Thoughts you should have RED-X'd out? What beliefs have made you doubt yourself, made you angry, held you back? Write them down, all the petty grudges that have rankled. How has your thinking about them, decades on, impacted on your life? If you didn't have those beliefs, those grudges, how different would life feel? Go through the list, RED-X the negatives and turn all those thoughts around, so we learn a positive lesson from each of them.

We shape and reshape our lives every day with how we feel about ourselves and others. Every day we place limitations on ourselves, hashing and rehashing old news, wasting energy on the negative, instead of looking for positive solutions. Look at that list – see how long it is. See its pattern weave itself through your life. With a little practice this RED-X becomes as automatic as flicking the indicator when driving. Detour to a positive thought, and straight away we correct our thinking. By controlling your thinking through my RED-X technique, your life will change – within days or weeks. It's a simple equation - when we think happy thoughts we experience more happiness. It's a great gift. Imagine being able to switch off your inner

63

critic, to instantly stop the thoughts that play over and over in our minds, robbing us of energy.

This technique requires persistence. I've written a SEVEN PART BUTTERFLY REMINDER for you. Its aim is to reinforce the Caterpillar technique daily, until you have changed your mindset.

1. Remember to do your self-relaxation for fifteen minutes every day. Remember to RED-X out negative thoughts then repeat the thought in a positive way.

2. RED-X out any negative phrases that others might say to you, repeating them to yourself in a positive way.

3. Remember to focus on what you want, not what you *don't* want.

4. Remember to do something every day that will take you closer to your day's goal.

5. Remember to praise yourself when you achieve your desired outcome for that day.

6. Remember to eat healthily, to give yourself energy.

7. Remember to be patient and kind to yourself and to be grateful for all the growth you have already experienced.

DO THE SEVEN PART BUTTERFLY
REMINDER EVERY DAY FOR 30 DAYS.
IF YOU FORGET, YOU MUST START ALL OVER AGAIN

Now you should be starting to make real changes in your life. Whilst you are practicing the RED-X technique, here are some other aspects of positive thinking we can use to turn our thinking around. Apply these principles on a daily basis.

If you really want to be happy, you must stop focusing on negative feelings. Start looking for the 'magical' feeling of happy, healthy functioning. That's a complicated way of saying everything feels OK. No judgements, no wishing things were different. Simple acceptance of reality.

If you asked 100 'happy people' the secret of their success, NONE of them would maintain that they never feel negative emotions, or experience negative thoughts. But virtually all of them would tell you that even in the midst of their negativity they trusted there was something better coming, that there were more important things happening than the negative feelings they were currently experiencing. They know that for every problem there is always a solution.

No one avoids problems in life. In fact, the stress they bring us can be good for us. The psychologist Carl Jung said, *'Man needs difficulties: they are necessary for health'*. Meeting and overcoming challenges is a *source* of psychological well-being. Positive energy will always beat negative energy – that means that healthy, positive thinking will outweigh any source of misery.

Once you begin to recognise healthy thinking it will become vital to your peace of mind. Discovering *your* level of healthy functioning is all you need to live a genuinely happy, productive life.

This process involves a degree of self-awareness. In other words, no more denying how we feel, but instead an honest acceptance of our emotions. It means learning what works against us, and what emotions sabotage us.

10

F.E.A.R.

What's most counterproductive to our happiness? What's the biggest INSTAR we face as we go through *The Butterfly Experience? Fear!*

Over the years patients have come to me demonstrating every possible condition as a result of stress. I've been asked to help alleviate the discomfort of terminal illness, improve infertility, I've treated patients with multiple sclerosis, spoken to people with almost every type of cancer and every form of anxiety. Every single condition arose out of fear. Fear is our biggest enemy – it is the enemy within.

Fear stops us growing. It makes us live small lives. Fear is learned behaviour. We are born without it. Negative experiences in childhood mean that from an early age we stop trusting. We become more self-sufficient in an effort to save ourselves pain. From infants who trust everyone, we go on to fear everything but our own instincts. But being human, we err, we fail ourselves. Now we know our own limitations. And so we buy into fear.

Fearful thoughts allowed to grow become real. We make them real. We feed them and keep them alive. We associate current happenings with painful memories of the past. Given enough energy and attention, our thoughts read like newspaper headlines. We catastrophise our thinking, until disasters lurk round every corner. Our confidence goes. And with our confidence goes opportunity. How often have you wanted to try something new and balked? How often have you wanted to speak to someone and walked away? What has fear cost you till now? And yet those of us living life free of fear understand that fear is just an illusion.

I have a neat acronym for FEAR. I call it 'False Emotions Appearing Real'. Fear is ugly, paralysing and corrosive. I want to show you how to turn fear around so it becomes a gift, a signal from your body to change things for the better.

Remember Pavlov's dog? Dr Ivan Pavlov was a Russian scientist who discovered that when he rang a bell for his dog to come for dinner, the dog would salivate. When he rang the bell the next day no dinner was offered, yet the dog still salivated. Pavlov realised it was a conditioned response. The dog had *assumed* the dinner would be there.

Fear is a conditioned response. What are you assuming when you are fearful? You are assuming certain things about yourself, your abilities and your limitations. I want you to become aware of that conditioned response, become aware of the racing heart, the sweaty palms, the signals your body is sending you.

We are reacting in that way because we have been *programmed* to act that way. Having learned the RED-X technique to eliminate our negative thoughts, we can go on to the next level. We can begin to break them down – identify them, name them, accept them. The next step is to change our reactions to them. That's freedom. By experiencing the willingness to try again, to look at things differently, we learn new behaviours, new thinking.

A quote by Nelson Mandela from his inaugural speech, taken from Marianne Williamson's book, *Return to Love: Reflections on the Principles of 'A Course in Miracles'* (HarperCollins. ©1992. First Edition.), shows there is another way to look at fear.

'Our biggest fear is not that we are inadequate. Our biggest fear is that we are powerful beyond measure. It is our light, not our darkness, that most frightens us. We ask ourselves, who am I to be brilliant, gorgeous, talented and fabulous?

You are a Child of God. Your playing small does not serve the world. There's nothing enlightened about shrinking so that other people won't be insecure around you. We were born to make magnificent the glory of God that is within us. It's not just in some of us, it is in everyone. And as we let our own light shine, we unconsciously give others permission to do the same. As we are liberated from our own fears, our presence automatically liberates others.'

Take a few minutes to sit and think about your own fears and anxieties. Be honest. A little bit of soul surgery is required here, so dig deep. Put the book down and come back to it when you're ready.

Overcoming fear

Take a few moments to try this following visualisation exercise to help you let go of fear and anxiety.

1. Sit in a comfortable position with your back straight. Allow your eyes to close. Breathe naturally and freely through your nose.

2. Allow yourself to float off to your favourite place where you feel safe and secure. Spend a little time identifying what it is you are currently afraid of. Is it the fear of dying? The fear of loss? The fear of failure? The fear of being found out? Name the fear. Say what it has done to you. Name the price you have paid.

3. Breathing easily, see yourself facing the fear. Look at yourself as if on a screen. Using your new ability to see things differently, understand that you have created this fear. See how your negative thinking has fed it. Own up to any part you have played in it. Sometimes fear comes as a result of guilt, because we are ashamed of our actions. Spend time with your Higher Self, feeling grateful for this realisation.

4. Visualise the fear. Watch yourself put all these fears in a pink balloon. Tie the balloon and send it skywards. Take a deep breath, blowing out any residue of fear. Say, 'I am willing and open to allowing any fears or anxiety to be released from my life.'

5. Inhale deeply. Imagine you are breathing in pure, inspiring energy. Surround your body with a white light of confidence and happiness. Feel this light pervade your whole body, through every cell and muscle.

6. Bring your mind back to the room.

7. Count up from 1 to 10, opening your eyes at the count of 8, feeling wide-awake.

After completing this exercise you will feel that your body and mind are completely clear of any fears and anxieties. Continue to do this exercise for one week, as reinforcement.

These two vital techniques, practiced faithfully, will catapult you to a better life. Here are some more Caterpillar tips to develop your spirit and emotions.

11

Seven Further Instars For Growth

INSTAR ONE

Look for the positive always. We are so conditioned to think in a negative way, that people go around looking for negatives that don't exist. Have you ever gone for an interview telling yourself you know you won't get it? And then not being surprised when your prophecy fulfils itself? Think in a positive manner at all times. It will shine through. The inverse also applies. *Only look for the positive,* no matter what the situation. There is always a solution to any problem - you just have to look for it.

This applies even when life takes a serious downswing. Often it takes drastic situations to really make you sit up and think. Say you've been made redundant from work. The negative approach wouldn't take long to find things to worry about - bills to pay, the loss of status. What about the opportunities that have just been handed to you? Finding a job that suits you better, one that will make you feel happier? See every problem as a challenge, a chance to change and step out the comfort zone.

INSTAR TWO

Stop negative thoughts as soon as you become aware of them, before they have a chance to grow. Remember to RED X them immediately and replace them with positive thoughts. Instead of telling yourself you can't do something, change it round. Tell yourself that of course you can do this, that you're getting stronger and stronger. *Stay away from negative thinkers.* Misery loves company. Negative people draw other negative people to themselves. If your friends are negative, then it's time to change who you spend your time with. Start thinking in a more positive manner and just watch the wonderful people you attract, vibrant, energetic, happy people who want the best for others. Are you a drainer? Then turn to a radiator for warmth and positive energy.

INSTAR THREE

Stop trying to do it all without help. *Connect to the Universe every day.* I can't stress enough the importance of a connection to the Spirit. It's the Source of all things for me. I know many of you are sceptical – I'm just asking you for now to try it. There's a whole chapter later on spirituality, our need for it and how to access it in your life. For today, ask for help, especially if times are difficult. That's when you need it most. Ask it to give you the courage and strength to go on. Or just ask it to lift your mood if you're feeling low. And if things are going well, ask it to direct you towards others you can help and be grateful.

INSTAR FOUR

Live in the Now. Your past is just a figment of your imagination, the future is a just a projection of the same. The only moment that is real is RIGHT NOW. It's a cliché, but tomorrow *is* the first day of the rest of your life. Live it with passion, live it honourably. Learning to trust your own body, and learning to trust yourself is not as difficult as you may think.

Next time you have to make a decision, mentally ask your body for a sign. First ask it the question and then *feel* how your body reacts. Some people feel it in their chest; I feel my body's response in my gut. I literally 'go with my gut' for all decisions.

The more you practice this vital skill, the healthier your thinking will be. The more often your body shows you the way forward, the more you will come to rely on it. Your ego may lie to you. Your body never does. Be proud of who you are.

INSTAR FIVE

Work at changing your own mindset, not the thinking of others. There are no two people the same. Even identical twins have their own fingerprints. Have you noticed that although identical twins have such similar personalities, one is always slightly happier, the other slightly sadder? It's like the two halves of the same coin. If identical twins can't be exactly like each other, how are we meant to achieve it? Yet we all try to have others think and act like us. The truth is we are all meant to have our own individual ideas and beliefs. We need to be different, because we all have a unique purpose and destiny.

INSTAR SIX

Think of people you know who try and control other people's lives. Why do they act that way, so domineering and manipulative? So bullying, even? The truth is they are trying to control their environment because their *own emotions are out of control.* They need to learn to relax, to let go, to accept others as they are. Don't accept attempts at controlling you. Stand up for yourself. Don't accept any behaviour that's unacceptable. In other words, don't be a doormat. Bullies sense a victim a mile away. Be yourself. Speak the truth. Others don't have to agree. But being true to yourself will win you respect.

INSTAR SEVEN

Work at creating sunshine in your life. Without fun, without laughter, life is a drudge. We all know individuals who moan constantly about their glass being half empty. But as Abraham Lincoln, sixteenth President of the United States said, 'Most of us are about as happy as we make up our minds to be'. Get proactive about your own happiness.

Stop right now and decide one thing that you will do today to brighten your day up. Arrange for a day off work. Meet an old friend. Buy yourself some fresh flowers. Take a walk in the park. Paint a picture and don't worry how it looks. Watch a favourite movie on DVD. *Remember to smile.* It helps your heart to stay happy. Be kind to

73

others but remember to be kind to yourself too.

Share your life with other people. Celebrate! Just enjoy being and trust in the process of life

Caterpillars are clued up. They use the natural gifts they have to avoid attack. They are careful, constantly aware of the predators around them. They develop cryptic colourings, which allow them to blend in. Caterpillars are constantly on the hunt for nourishment, driven by the need to grow.

Hunger for life has allowed them to develop a key skill - the ability to distinguish chemical signatures. In other words, they know what to avoid. Sometimes we have to learn *whom* to avoid.

This chapter is all about energy. I want to teach you about good energies and energies we have to keep away from. No matter where we are, we are open to other people's energy. It is so important that we protect ourselves from negative energy. Would you sneeze and not use a handkerchief? Then why would you allow other people's negative energy to surround you?

How many times have you felt fantastic and met someone and then felt really drained. Each day on awakening, I shower. While dressing I mentally put on a blue velvet cloak. I do this to protect myself from my clients' negative energy in order to not get drained. I only take off my cloak when I retire to bed. It's important to keep it on mentally - even with your own family.

They too have problems and negativity. You can take ideas on board. Choose a blue velvet cloak, or imagine a glass jar over your body. Some people prefer to think of a healthy glow, or a golden light surrounding their body as protection. You do what is right for you.

I've written seven tasks that follow on from here to help you focus on energy fundamentals. From today I want you to practice them, becoming more aware of your energy and the energy of others. Focus on each specific task. Allow yourself to understand what it is you seek from yourself.

'The higher your energy level, the more efficient your body. The more efficient your body, the better you feel and the more you will use your talent to produce outstanding results'

Anthony Robbins

TASK ONE

Set a good, positive foundation by staying within your natural character – understand your strengths and don't try to become a clone of anyone else. Embrace your gifts and work on your confidence.

TASK TWO

Focus on what you want to happen. Use positive thinking every day to see the outcomes you want in life. Bring them alive, so your subconscious feels as though these good things have already happened.

TASK THREE

Remember to protect yourself against negative people. Avoid reading newspapers filled with toxic stories and watching garbage on the television. Be aware of the energy around you. Stop trying to 'read' other people's thoughts. You are responsible only for your own.

TASK FOUR

Make a conscious decision to only be around positive people. Surround yourself with positive energy. Read positive books and listen to upbeat music that will lift your vibrations. Seek the good in other people – presume the best in them. Everyone is doing their best.

TASK FIVE

Be aware of your body language and how it can affect others. We wear our pain on the outside and people pick up on it. We can 'fake it to make it' until our improved thinking automatically improves the way we are around others.

TASK SIX

Never give up and always believe in your dream. Persistence is the key to success in all areas of life. There is always a solution, you just have to find it. Get creative. Open yourself up to new ideas.

TASK SEVEN

Never accept NO for an answer. Always try, try and try again. Richard Branson says that although he listens with care to others, he still relies on himself and makes up his own mind.

Now that you understand the process of INSTAR, you can practice it daily and grow daily. But how do we grow enough to get to the next place?

What clarity do you have in your life? Is your vision hazy or is it very clear? Do you know what you desire? Do you believe it will happen? These are just some of the questions you need to be asking yourself.

How do we use *The Butterfly Experience* to move to the next level of emotional, financial and spiritual security? Let's get you there by using the three Cs of the Caterpillar.

12

Trusting The Three Cs –
Commitment, Courage, Control

Commitment

We make a *commitment* to move forward in life. We have the *courage* to take that next step. We stay in *control* of our lives.

The Dalai Lama, in his advice for meditation, states '...in your life, unless you make specific time for something that you feel committed to, you will always have other obligations and you will always be too busy.'

To be truly successful at anything, you need commitment. Commitment isn't something you can pretend to have, because you'll soon be found out. Commitment comes through belief.

Make a commitment today to regularly visualise the new, more positive YOU. Make a commitment to dream of the success that is headed your way. Make a commitment to really bin the old plan, the one where you just waited for something to happen. Make a conscious effort to spend real time, invest real energy in deciding what you want from life.

Committing to a goal often means giving up other things, making sacrifices. It sometimes means admitting that the old way we've been doing things hasn't worked. It means looking for new strategies. Keep your mind focused on what's important. Set your goals. Prioritise, but be realistic about what you can achieve. Visualise yourself doing what you want to do – visualise yourself practicing those actions. Commit to happiness, to finding and following your true purpose. Each and every sacrifice will be worth it.

There are those in life who make things happen, those who watch things happen, and those who say, 'What happened?' You can sit around admiring the beautiful butterfly. Or you can start today to make changes so that you can be a butterfly too.

Unless we commit ourselves to focusing on something that fulfils us, life can just seem to pass us by. We waste our lives waiting for them to start. Commit daily to what you are trying to achieve. When we do, we're rewarded. And that's a feeling you can't buy.

Courage

We have examples of courage all around us – children with terminal illnesses who want to make life better for others. Whole nations showing tremendous bravery. Recognise that living the life you're destined to live will take a little courage.

Courage involves self-awareness, being honest with yourself. It means stepping out your comfort zone, remembering that you can always return there if you have to. When we've found the courage to take that first, difficult step, most people discover how fantastic it feels when we stretch ourselves. We discover how amazing it is to experience living in the moment.

How much courage do you have currently in your mindset? I want you to go within yourself, right now, and ask yourself that question. Ask yourself, how free do you want to be? How small does your life have to get before you can find it within you to break out of that prison you've made for yourself? Do you have enough courage to start thinking positively? DO IT NOW.

Control

Here's one of the great paradoxes of positive thinking – in order to be in control of our lives, we have to relinquish control. The need for control is negative thinking – its damage limitation. It's an insidious weed we need to eradicate. When we do our lives are enriched, calmer, happier and healthier.

Why is it that people are so afraid to let go? I see people with control issues time and time again in my practice.

78

Often patients are unwilling to admit their controlling behaviour or are totally unaware of it. Many of my patients have responsible positions – psychiatrists, doctors, nursing sisters, teachers, managers, directors. They come to see me for stress and are horrified when I tell them they've created the stress themselves, by trying to control others. When they learn to control their own thoughts and emotions, they take back control of their life. There is less stress and anxiety. They learn to relax.

'I cannot trust a man to control others who cannot control himself'
Robert E. Lee

This alone gives us a tremendous feeling of security and happiness. Releasing negative thoughts of others frees us. It allows us to devote time to what we want in life, and how to achieve it. It is our birthright to be happy in life. When we let go of our fears and stop trying to control others then we become happier.

If you can admit that life is not what you would like it to be, then that itself is a start. It is the *beginning* of a new way of thinking. Carrying around negative thoughts of others makes us unhappy and dispirited. Imagine if you could let go of your negative thoughts? Imagine not caring how others perceived you? Well you can! We can release the anxieties. Our mind becomes lighter and clearer. We can go forward with confidence.

Having gone through the process of shedding, let's focus now on what we need to take us beyond this stage. Remember it's all about learning and growing, and possibly getting rid of some bad habits.

This next section focuses on energy boosters we can bring into our lives easily and effectively.

****

BUTTERFLY BODY LANGUAGE TECHNIQUES

Here are some proven techniques on making a good first impression – often overlooked and so easy to rectify.

It's a fact: employers promote based on body language. Through becoming more aware of your own body language, but also through recognising the body language of others, you can develop your own self-esteem and change how others think about you. People want to know – what kind of a person am I dealing with here? You might feel your speech does that, but your body language gives people far more information about us. From it they know if you're confident or insecure, quiet or extrovert. Whether you're the kind of person people listen to.

We all interpret body language all the time on a subconscious level. We start forming impressions of people we meet from the moment we set eyes on them. A huge part of the first impression you create comes from your body language. Your posture, facial expression, eye contact, and gestures speak louder than anything you say.

It's vital to use your energy to make a positive impression, even if we feel like a marshmallow inside. By holding your back straight, your head up and dressing in a confident way. Neat and tidy hair is a must, as is a welcoming smile. All these simple things go a long way to making us look positive even if we don't feel it. The secret is in looking confident and, by so doing, we will start to act and behave in that way. Others will respect us.

What about our bodies? Your face is easily the most easy-to-read part of the body. Your expression can make you look bored or animated, interested or frankly turned off. Make a conscious effort to smile at people. Being able to smile easily and warmly is a simple gift we can give ourselves.

Focus on your smile over the next few days, especially when meeting new people. Make a conscious effort to smile. Your smile is one of the strongest tools you have. It makes us look friendly, open and warm.

Our eyes tell people how we're really feeling. It's hard to hide our emotions if we give eye contact. That's why people like it and why they distrust those who find eye contact difficult. What are we hiding, they want to know. Don't overcompensate. A direct stare can be very intimidating. It implies intensity. Making very little eye contact can either convey shyness or submissiveness. Aim for the middle ground – holding people's eyes for a short while. It tells others you are at ease.

Direct eye contact is of the utmost importance. It builds trust.

Your hands also express the inner you. Fidgeting makes everyone aware of how nervous you are feeling. Constantly touching your clothes or face can make you look anxious and even false. Try and use open gestures – they show honesty. Keep them moderate – no big windmill movements. You can express enthusiasm and commitment without knocking over vases. Big gestures make you appear out of control.

Pay attention to how you shake someone's hand. Handshakes should not be too hard and not too soft. An upright, firm handshake is usually best. Power handshakes are to be avoided – people instinctively know you are trying to dominate from the onset.

Your posture more than anything conveys your level of self-confidence. When we are feeling less than assured we hunch our shoulders. Even if you feel nervous, force those shoulders back and try to adopt a more advanced stance. Turn towards people as you are speaking to them. Interested people always pay attention and lean forward. Leaning backwards demonstrates aloofness or rejection. Standing too far away seems standoffish. Try and judge people's personal space. It's easy to step over the mark and intimidate people.

By helping your posture you work on your self-belief. In the morning take a few moments to write down three positive Butterfly Affirmations that you want to believe about yourself. Each day of our lives take a few precious minutes to affirm positive Butterfly Affirmations about yourself. As you say them, retrain your mind. For example:

- I believe I am powerful
- I believe I am successful
- I believe I am confident

Try it and see the difference!

In summary, our body language betrays what's happening inside us. It says whether what we're saying is consistent with what's happening with our emotions. Being aware of our body language lets us send out good messages about ourselves and raises our self-confidence. Here are some examples of how colour can enhance your confidence and your body language.

CATERPILLAR COLOURS

Colours are important, an easy way to boost the way we feel. Each colour has its own wavelength and frequency. In this Caterpillar phase I want you to become aware of the colours you wear and the colours in your environment. Subconsciously we pick up on colour messages all the time. Here's a small indication of how colours can affect our moods and the moods of those around us. Caterpillars use them to advantage.

Red helps to assert authority. It will make you feel confident and give you an energy boost.

It is said to be the colour of love and helps stimulate your heartbeat. It is a passionate colour. Use red in your home to manifest abundance. Wearing it makes you look vital, alive.

Green helps you to concentrate and be more focused. This is one of the most popular colours for people painting a room. It is a very calming colour. It helps focus and vision. Green makes people think you are friendly, a team player, and well balanced.

Blue will also calm you in times of stress. Wear it if you want to look or seem serene. The body will actually produce calming chemicals. We can feel cold in a blue room. Looking at the colour blue stimulates the thyroid and that affect your heart, bones, hair and reproductive organs. Verbal ability is improved when we wear blue. If you're going to negotiate something, wear navy. It makes you look trustworthy.

Purple is a good brain booster. Good when you are doing brainstorming. It is said to be a romantic and feminine colour. Purple makes people think you are ethical and high-minded. Purple helps us be more intuitive and connects us to a Higher Consciousness.

Yellow is cheerful. People who wear it are considered optimists. Think of Spring and daffodils. Yellow enhances concentration. Wear it if you need to do analytical work. It is said to be a holistic colour.

Orange is hot and vibrant. We think of brightly coloured clothes. It is a hot and spicy colour. If you want to stand out in a room, wear orange. Orange for many is the colour of happiness. It promotes energy and focus. Orange makes you look enthusiastic about life.

Gold is aligned with masculine power, and silver – reminiscent of the moon – denotes feminine energy.

Now that you know how to give yourself a quick colour boost, perhaps you could combine colour energy with my suggestions for improved body language. But be aware. None of these things can disguise a poor...

ATTITUDE

How's your attitude? Be completely honest now. Rate yourself out of ten. Do you stomp around at work moaning all day? Are you the one whose moods people tip toe around? Do you complain constantly – or do people say you are a breath of fresh air? Perhaps you are somewhere in between?

Start thinking today about your attitude, in the family and at work. What you put into life you'll get back tenfold. Do you pull your weight at work, or sit back waiting for some other fool to volunteer? Do you think the world owes you a living?

The best way I know to improve my own attitude is self-acceptance. Accept yourself the way you are and work to improve what you feel would advance you. Being happy is an inside job. Peace of mind comes from knowing we've done our best. That way we don't need praise from others to make us happy. When you believe in yourself you give off a positive self-image. Just by looking at you people know you have clear ideas and know where you are going in life. You stand out.

Attitude tells most keenly when we're challenged. In my first marriage my husband was made redundant twice in the space of one year. He could have gone to pieces and broken down. But the situation made him look at other options in life and start to retrain in education.

I recently met someone who had just been made redundant from his job. He was positively radiant, happy to have been given an opportunity to start investing in another company. He had put all his energy into this new venture.

Think of a challenging time in your life. Think how you handled it. Would you do the same today?

We learn and we grow. When we feel good about who we are then we can look at life's difficulties in different ways. WHICH ONE ARE YOU? When we have a positive attitude then we are half way to achieving our goals. We feel and look better, more confident and are happier with ourselves.

The strong, confident person looks at an obstacle in a challenging way, looking for new opportunities to grow. Caterpillars can fall off a leaf many times, but they always climb back up again.

Tom Hunter, the millionaire Scottish entrepreneur says, 'We have opportunities every day of our lives, it's knowing which ones will make us successful'. Using that gut intuition. I have always looked at challenges as new opportunities and there is always a solution in every problem, we just need to learn to look and be open to it. You should have an air of expectancy around you, looking for great things to happen.

13

Caterpillar Self Care

Often one of the things that we most dislike about ourselves is the unhealthy habits we indulge in. The caterpillar stage is where we shed unhealthy habits – stopping smoking for example, or dumping the idea that you don't need to exercise. By changing the way you think you'll begin to look fabulous on the outside.

Caterpillars know all things are good in moderation. Having a glass of wine with your meal is acceptable. But often it leads to two or three. Before you know it the bottle is empty. Don't over-indulge in alcohol. It leaves the body feeling low and depressed. At first you may feel relaxed but if you continue to drink then you start to get moody. Alcohol is a toxin.

The same goes for smoking. People who smoke have a tougher skin surface. The skin on their fingers goes yellow in colour. Imagine the damage they are doing on the inside. Drugs are the same.

Caterpillars know that avoiding substances that are not good for the body is the only way to live a long and healthy life.

What age do you feel? What age are you really? Do they match? Take a moment to think about how you treat your body. Poor diet, stodgy food, lack of fresh air. For so long your body has accepted mental and physical abuse – and all self-imposed.

The Caterpillar stage is where we say we're no longer going to accept the way we've been treating ourselves. You wouldn't treat an animal that way, so why do it to yourself?

Our Butterfly Blueprint is determined to a degree by the body we have and how we look after it. This section will discuss several pressing health problems and offer a prescription for health. I believe that we have the ability to heal ourselves and I want to help you get in touch with your Butterfly Energy.

'I am part of all that I have met'

Lord Tennyson

14

Energy And Health

Everything in life is energy. The world is *filled* with energy. We are energy, the plants, food, our furniture, it's all *energy*. Energy is all around us. Energy lies within us all. That means that we all have the power within us to choose and create our own life. We live in an energy field. Where does that energy come from? We take it in through food and the air around us, but also from other people.

Intuitively we pick up on emotional impressions, almost without being aware of it. We avoid certain people instinctively. When someone comes too close and steps in 'your space', you feel their energy.

Some people we trust naturally. Others repel us, we feel the tension immediately. Why is it that we like some people and not others? It has to do with energy. We all know someone that makes us feel low, lacking in confidence, who drains us. That's our energy seeping out to them. You can even feel someone's fear, if that is the energy they are giving out.

Alternatively we know the energy we love to feel when we are preparing to go on holiday. We are on a high and feel wonderful. You can feel the energy at a rock concert or watching your favourite group. The support act is brought on to build up the energy and get the audience warmed up before the main attraction comes on.

By the time the band comes on stage the energy in the stadium is electric. You can feel it. That's energy. And that's the feel good factor we get when we harness this power.

The Dalai Lama is small in stature, but he has a magnificent, wonderful energy. When he walks into the room you can *feel* his joy. Despite all the sorrow and injustice he has encountered, he remains compassionate and resilient. He has never forgotten his life purpose – to serve others. These qualities have made him one of the greatest leaders of this world.

Can you think of a time you went for an interview? Relive that moment. Feel the energy in the room. Either it felt relaxed or it felt unpleasant. That feeling comes from the people in the room. It is their energy. You can pick up on it. Sense it. When we feel sad or even below par, our friends and family notice. We give out a different energy. I remember speaking to a Head Teacher who told me that he referred to his staff as radiators and drainers. He simply meant that some people's energy is boiling hot, they are very positive and energetic. You can feel their energy. Then there are the others we all know - the ones who suck us dry. These are the people that make us feel tired at the end of the day, what we call *'drained of energy'*.

When you believe in yourself then you have an inner confidence and you radiate confidence. Thoughts are energy. When you think about the whales in the ocean they can detect energy movement and sound many miles away from the object.

Think of the ocean as a vast electric bath. Full of powerful energy and yet we can be soothed and feel relaxed listening to the ocean waves lapping to and fro. Invisible energy helps us to live our life. Sometimes there are just no explanations why things happen and how they happen.

We have to learn to trust in the process of life. *Anything can happen if you let it.* Opportunities arise and unusual events happen and we sometimes can't explain how. When we are working and flowing with universal energy then good things seem to happen.

When we swim against the universal energy flow then the events just keep getting worse. We sleep in for work, the car breaks down, and everything just seems to happen at once. Ever wondered why? When we think in a positive manner then our energy changes. We attract people with the same vibrations. When our energy is up then everything seems to be fine. Success just keeps on bringing success. Things just always go right. So why not learn to tune into it, work with it, benefit from it?

For thousands of years, human beings have been aware of the holistic health benefits of working with healing energy. Energy is all around us and works in so many different ways. Think of the electricity that comes from water, the sheer power of it. Envisage the energy that goes into delivering a baby. Remember the energy of a wedding day, the joy that was created around the happy couple.

Now think of the person who commits a murder - the energy and anger transmitted from that person. Energy is a wonderful tool but it must be used wisely.

It doesn't matter what religion or cultural background we come from, we all have the ability to use our own healing energy, balancing the subtle energies within and around our bodies. The medical profession is baffled by it, but even its more conservative elements have begun to be more open to it.

If we have an imbalance in our bodies then our energies are out of kilter. Eventually, if left untreated, that imbalance will manifest itself into some sort of illness. The solution is simple. We need to listen to our bodies, to communicate with them. But most of us have become so reliant on medication and intervention we have forgotten how to read what our bodies are signalling.

Where do these imbalances come from? Over our lifetime we accumulate so much baggage. Most of us should be walking around followed by a removals truck, Regrets R Us. The sad part is we *believe* all those negative beliefs that we have collected about ourselves, family, friends and society. This negative energy is what creates imbalances in our energy field and aura, causing illness and disease.

Neither fame nor wealth nor talent can make us immune to negative energy. Judy Garland had the most wonderful voice. She was born to entertain. Her energy lit up the stage. Sadly the wonderful energy she had as a child began to change. Judy seemed to attract the wrong partners. She developed other problems, including alcohol dependency and physical abuse. Judy's life, which started out so full of promise, spiralled deeper and deeper into despair. Photographs and film footage of her in her later years are so sad - her energy is sending out a help signal. At the age of 47 she died from barbiturate poisoning. The coroner's verdict was accidental death. I believe she died of a broken spirit.

Negative energy is a form of self-abuse, a habit, which can be unlearned. The good news is, as with self-relaxation, we can learn new skills. We are *all* energy channels. That means we can heal our own bodies. I have witnessed so many examples of people healing themselves using their own energy, belief and determination to live. And I want to teach you to do the same.

We've already spoken about how we activate our own healing using energy fields. Meditation taps into our ability to self-heal. When we do our self-relaxation, we tap into Kundalini energy. Kundalini is a Sanskrit word that means 'snake'. The body has seven energy chakras. Chakra is a Sanskrit word meaning wheel and it refers to the seven energy centres in our body. These energy wheels regulate the flow of energy through our energy system. These centres open and close when we decide what to think and when we feel. Our spiritual energy is like a snake all coiled up inside our base chakra, which can rise right up to our crown chakra. Kundalini is the life force, the energy in our spirit body known in China as chi, in India as prana and in Japan as ki. Kundalini flows through our body.

When we tap into this Kundalini energy we feel re-energised, calmer and more positive.

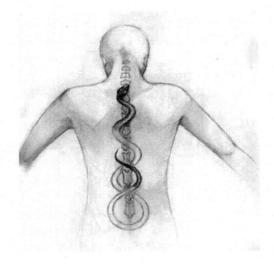

Kundalini Chakras
http://www. crystalinks.com/chakras.html

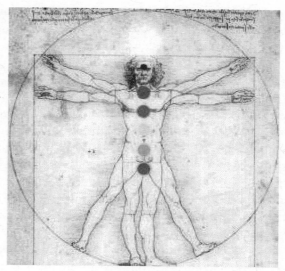

Kundalini Chakras
http://www. crystalinks.com/chakras.html

In the Caterpillar stage you still have many obstacles to overcome. You've made a tremendous start by recognising negative thinking patterns. Now I want you to consider some other predators that will try and steal your peace of mind.

NEGATIVITY OF OTHERS

Think of the people you know who are happy and content – do they fight and rail at circumstance or do they make the best of it? People who are *in control* of their lives are high energy people, motivated, constantly eager to learn and grow. You need to be in control. When you believe in the process of life, that everything happens for a purpose, then uncanny events happen. Every day we are faced with a different challenge. The real difference – the road less travelled – is in how we deal with them. Are you calm, focused and positive? Or are you sending out stress signals and negative energy?

We all know people who are hyper-stressed. They lurch from one crisis to the next, nervous and bad tempered. No matter what the situation, they look at it negatively, seeing problems as unsolvable. Unhappy, they insist on sharing their unhappiness with others. Some even resort to anger or bullying others. Sound familiar?

STRESS

How stressed are you? We all need a certain amount of stress to feel good, but too much stress can and will affect your health – literally make you feel *distressed*. Stress manifests itself in so many ways – in our physical reactions, in our emotions and responses. When we think of stress we tend to think of going for an interview, the death of a partner, an unannounced visit by the mother-in-law. But stress affects us every day, in dozens of minor ways. Its compound effect is devastating. So before you have a breakdown on your way to a wedding or walk out on your job, we need to recognise stress and deal with it. Stress shows itself in different ways, is unique to every person. When we understand stress and how it affects us we can choose to lead a healthier lifestyle and take precautions against it. Most of us think that stress equals worry. But most of us carry emotional stress without even knowing it.

How is your energy level, right now, this minute? Do you wake up each day with a smile on your face, ready for the new day ahead? Or do you wish you could go back to bed? Do you seek a solution for every problem? Or do you give up, finding life too hard? Do you run out of energy half way through every race? Do you hate confrontation? Do you avoid difficult conversations, either in the boardroom or at home? Do you avoid making decisions, for fear of making the wrong ones?

Stress makes us feel as though we're suffocating, whether it's in the family or at work. It doesn't have to be that way. Begin the process of change with a decision. Start *now*. Find time to heal your self. Decide what needs to change in order to get rid of any imbalances we have created over the years. No one likes 'change', but to grow we need constant changes. The secret is believing that change doesn't have to be stressful. It can be as easy or as hard as you like. You decide. You're in control.

When we change the colour of our hair or begin to lose weight, for example. At first we feel out of our comfort zone. Then people compliment us and tell us we look good. We start to feel good and act in a confident manner, behave in a confident way. At first you felt funny, not quite yourself. Now you feel fantastic and wondered how you could have ever had your hair that old colour or allowed that weight to remain. It is quite remarkable just how quickly we adjust to 'change'.

Think again of what you really want to 'change'. Something that will challenge you and take you out of your comfort zone. Do you want to change your shape? Do you want to change your look? No matter what 'changes' you make, you will feel at first out of your comfort zone. But very quickly self-acceptance creeps in. Notice how quickly you feel in control and fabulous.

BAD EATING HABITS

Especially in this caterpillar section it's vital that we nourish ourselves well.

Caterpillars are eating machines, devouring everything in their path that will help them move through this process as quickly as possible. They can multiply in size either quickly or slowly, depending on how quickly they get hold of what they need. Feeding off the nutrients it finds, it wanders from place to place, looking for a safe place to begin the next phase in its transformation.

How can we look healthy, feel energetic and have that glow on the outside if our bodies are full of rubbish on the inside? Do you eat for comfort to get through life?

The body needs constant repair. Like a car, our body breaks down when we don't look after it. Fill a car up with the wrong petrol and we get 'kangaroo jumps'. If we fill our body up with wrong things, we get a bad reaction. Nutrition is key to our well-being, physically and mentally. We have to nourish our bodies with healthy food. Otherwise our bodies and minds will become run down, and finally break down.

Nutrition plays an important role in healing. Often when I see patients the first thing I ask them to do is detoxify the body. We look at foods which will increase their energy and restore the body to a more alkaline base. Once the physical side is taken care of, we move towards the mental and emotional sides of their healing. In my experience, no matter what problem patients present with, if they improve their mindset about nutrition, every aspect of their health improves.

People forget sometimes that food isn't there simply for our pleasure. Food is nourishment. It's a necessity for our physical well-being. The quality of the food we eat has an immediate impact on our health. A car can't run without petrol. So why do we think our body can be energised with no food or the wrong kind of food? When we feed our body with the right food, we feel stronger. Our mood improves - we are less irritable as our body benefits from better digestion. We have the energy to achieve our goals.

'Not what we have but what we enjoy constitutes abundance'
Epicurus

Forget fad diets. Eating well needs to be a far greater priority for most of us. Instead of resorting to high-sugar snacks that give us a false sense of energy, think nutrition. With a little thought and a positive mindset, turning our diet around can make all the difference between low energy and the quality of life we're aiming for. Love your body. Eat well. Eat everything in moderation. You'll soon start to see the difference.

We have to assess what we are feeding our body on a daily basis. Avoid caffeine and sugary snacks.

Sugar stimulates a brain chemical which is called beta endorphin. This is the same brain chemical affected by morphine and heroin. Sugar gives us a feeling of euphoria and wellness but it soon wears off, leaving us angry and irritable. This is called withdrawal. If you continue to take more sugar then it will relieve your feelings but it continues the cycle, the nutritional Catch 22. Sugar is actually tricking the brain into thinking it is helping and alleviating the symptoms. In fact it is making you feel worse.

Sugar turns into fat. We pile on the weight thinking that the chocolate bars are helping relieve our pain. What we need is to be in control of our emotions. Sugar makes them out of control. Ditto the caffeine we take every day. Everything in moderation.

A cup of coffee becomes a crutch. Start your day with a healthy fruit juice. Coffee often causes a drastic 'gut reaction'. Your body doesn't lie. It knows what foods and substances are bad for it. Listen to what it's telling you.

THE FRESHLY HATCHED CATERPILLAR IS VERY SOFT AND VULNERABLE.

Caterpillars are careful about what they feed their bodies. Good food is made up of different types of nutrients. Here's a quick run down, so you can see just how important they are.

Vitamin A is essential for the eyes. It helps us maintain our night vision and helps us to see the world in colour. Without sufficient vitamin A, blindness can occur. Vitamin A is found in apricots, pumpkin, eggs and carrots.

Vitamin B helps our body make energy. It is involved in making red blood cells which carry the oxygen around our body. Every single part of our body needs oxygen. Those of us who suffer from low moods probably need more vitamin B in our diet. Eat more beans and alfalfa sprouts, whole grains, oats, parsley and seaweed.

Vitamin C helps our body tissue, like our muscles, to stay healthy. It helps any cuts and wounds to heal. It is also good for keeping colds at bay. Vitamin C is found in oranges, red and green peppers, lemons, tomatoes and cabbage.

Vitamin D helps our body make strong bones. Vitamin D is found in milk, salmon and eggs. Regular sunlight is vital to help the body take in vitamin D, although of course it is important to protect our bodies from too much sun.

Vitamin E helps other body tissues such as our eyes and skin stay healthy. It also helps to protect our lungs from damage from air pollutants. It helps make red blood cells. Vitamin E is found in sardines, nuts and green spinach.

Vitamin K helps our blood clot. It helps to stop the blood flow. Vitamin K is found in pork, liver and yoghurt.

Magnesium is an excellent supplement for the brain. It helps memory and is wonderful for boosting the immune system. When a patient has been diagnosed with cancer I ask them to start taking this supplement.

Of course, there are so many other nutrients. Calcium, for example, is important in helping build our bones and teeth and can be found in dairy products, tofu and cabbage.

Sodium helps regulate the fluid balance of our bodies. It aids the contraction and expansion of muscles. It is present in all our body fluids. Sodium is found in the vegetable zucchini and is also found in salt.

Iron is needed for the development of our brains. It is especially important that we get enough iron from the ages of 6 month to 2 years. After 6 months of age a child only gets 50% of the iron it needs from breast milk. The balance has to be made up in the child's diet. If we don't have enough iron then we can become anaemic.

The iron in your body is used to make haemoglobin. This is vital as the haemoglobin carries oxygen around the body. Haemoglobin is the substance that makes your red blood cells red. When your cells are bright red then they have lots of oxygen. They turn a bluish colour when they have off-loaded their oxygen to cells round your body.

This is why the blood going from your heart out to your body, in your arteries, is bright red, and the blood coming back, in your veins, has a bluish tinge. Look at the veins on the back of your hand.

Iron that is not being used is stored. If your body doesn't make enough haemoglobin then you become anaemic. You get tired, you lack concentration. In severe cases you may even experience breathlessness. In other words, your body isn't getting enough oxygen. Most cases of anaemia can be treated by taking an iron supplement, but it is always important to consult your doctor. Let the professionals diagnose your condition and measure how much haemoglobin you have in your blood.

The best source of iron is found in red meat and fish which can easily be absorbed but there are other foods that have iron - baked beans, wholemeal bread, wheat cereals, white bread and prunes. You see, we don't have to buy expensive meals to improve our health. We can eat well even though we are on a budget. You don't have to spend a lot to enjoy a healthy lunch. What about a rainbow salad of different vegetables? Why absorb vitamins in tablet form when we can have that goodness from fresh fruit and vegetables? Enjoy tuna sandwiches with ripe tomatoes. Or try snacking on sunflower seeds, mixed nuts and raisins – what could be better for a mid-afternoon snack? Choose a piece of fruit. Peaches are packed with vitamins and give a great energy boost.

And in the evenings use simple rice - mix carrots and chicken through it. Add some pineapple and mango. Get creative. A pot of soup with all the goodness from the vegetables and pulses can last two days and be very economical with crusty bread. Or make a pot of pasta. Add some fresh tomatoes and mushrooms *et voilà*! A healthy and nutritious meal in minutes. Salmon slices sprinkled with peppers and cooked in the oven for 20 minutes, served with some sweet red potatoes and some broccoli – heaven! Fish is a good source of brain power – we should eat it two or three times a week.

Cook organic lamb and add beans for nutrition. Serve with either pasta or potatoes and some seasonal vegetables. Or what about baked beans on toast covered with melted cheese? Cheap and nutritious.

Remember you are growing from a caterpillar into a beautiful butterfly!

MAKE A CONSCIOUS EFFORT TODAY TO EAT HEALTHILY.
GIVE YOUR BODY A CHANCE.

It's not just *what* we eat, but *how* we eat that's important. Also, most people eat too quickly. Eating slowly helps us to enjoy our food, so that we can be alert for the signal our body sends us, saying it is sated. It has been proven that when people eat slowly they take in fewer calories and have a greater feeling of fullness. The body is better able to take in nutrients if they are well chewed – less strain on the body. Chewing is better for your digestion, which means you don't have cramps or indigestion afterwards.

It is important to heed your body signals. Don't continue eating when your body is saying it's had enough – unless you want to feel bloated. After months and years of overeating our stomach gradually expands to allow more capacity. Again a vicious cycle is onset – bigger stomach means we can eat more and more, without feeling full.

Caterpillars eat well but are constantly on the move. Remember to eat small, frequent meals rather than one large meal a day. Eat small

97

bites and chew your food well. Remain upright for thirty minutes after eating, in order to allow gravity to aid digestion. Don't go to bed on a full stomach. Don't eat after 8.30pm. It's harder for any food to be digested. Relax. Stress produces stomach acid.

Eat fast food - foods that will pass through your stomach quickly rather than foods that will hang around in the stomach, such as high fat foods. Blend fruit. Make yogurt smoothies with it. Blend vegetables into nourishing soups that will pass through the stomach quickly. This is particularly good for patients who are unwell, minimising the chance of reflux. I ask my cancer patients to start using a juicer as this will help to energise their body and change the acidity in the body. They will feel less tired and will gain energy from all the fresh fruit. I juice every day of my life.

Drink plenty of water. This is one of the most important things you can do for your body. It flushes the toxins out of the body and helps to purify your blood. It can take several weeks to properly rehydrate a body. Most of us are dehydrated and don't even know it. Dehydration can also feel like hunger, so we eat instead of taking water into our system. The body is further burdened trying to break down more food.

WEIGHT

For many people weight is an issue. Being overweight often hides emotions that are out of control. Whether we can admit it or not, excess weight usually means we are repressing emotional issues. We're either bingeing to comfort ourselves, or choosing unhealthy foods that fail to nourish our bodies. Food becomes a control or coping mechanism. We eat rather than deal with our emotional baggage. Unless there is a physical problem that causes the excess weight, our body is trying to communicate emotional distress. What people see on the outside is a mirror image of how we feel on the inside. People don't comment on weight – it's considered rude. But because of our reluctance to address the issue, people don't get the help they need.

Some of us use food in a different way, trying not to eat at all. Their lack of self worth spirals into an eating disorder. People who suffer with anorexia find security in controlling an aspect of their lives – until they almost kill themselves. They soothe their soul by punishing their body.

The way you eat is your way of coping with life. If you are severely over or underweight, you are not coping with your emotions. Your body is crying out, but you don't hear it. When we ignore our emotions we are invalidating our pain, saying it's not real. We think we should cope, be stronger than we are. But we are actually making our pain worse by holding it inside. It won't go away. It just gets worse. Repressed pain manifests itself as disease and discomfort. When we believe in ourselves, we mirror that image to the world. The image you portray is a mirror image of who you are on the inside. What does your image say to the world?

Weight is a huge issue and could be a book on its own. To be healthy and live a good life we do have to be aware of our body and listen to what it says. Just by eating nutritious food and taking regular exercise you can start to lead a healthy life. You don't need to waste money on diets that don't work. As soon as you start to go back to your old ways again, the weight goes right back on. Work out what your triggers are. Use a food diary to see how your emotions are causing you to seek comfort in food. A food diary also helps us work out which foods we have a history of overeating.

Too many people try to heal on their own. I want to stress here the importance of finding support and encouragement. We need to surround ourselves with people who understand and don't judge. Look for solutions – be with people who have found the way out. When we open our hearts to the universe and become willing to change we are half way to healing. Just be open to new ideas.

INSOMNIA

Poor dietary habits are just one way we rob ourselves of energy. Disturbed sleep is another. The amount we require depends on our age. Most children need twelve hours a day. Deepak Chopra tells us that children sleep so well because they have no worries or anxieties. Their minds are free from stress. Adults function best on around seven or eight hours, a huge percentage of the population survives on far less. As adults our sleep is disturbed by negative thinking. We sabotage our sleep reserves, depriving ourselves of rest, torturing ourselves with what ifs and why nots? Surveys show one in three Britons suffer from insomnia at one time or another.

People who suffer with insomnia usually have 'racing' minds. The brain is simply unable to shut down and heal itself. Sleeplessness has become a national epidemic. It has terrible consequences, at work, in our relationships, and on our economy. Motorists fall asleep at the wheel due to overwork and stress. Instead of taking 'ME' time and learning to relax, people are literally driving on 'empty', causing terrible accidents.

People who suffer trauma go into a coma - deep sleep. This is the body's way of healing itself. It has been shut down by the mind, in order for it to heal. Sleep is the great healer. So if you have problems sleeping this is where we identify how you can help yourself. And I'm not talking about pills. No one should have to be on long-term medication for insomnia. And that's not just my opinion.

'About 85 per cent of people who have insomnia can be helped with a combination of behavioural therapy and medicine. Insomnia has traditionally been viewed as a symptom of an underlying medical or psychiatric illness, and drugs to treat insomnia are approved for short-term use only, until the *primary condition* can be treated' *(my emphasis in italics)*.

Marc Raphaelson, M.D., Neurologist

I can understand why people pop pills – it is out of desperation. Our bodies need sleep. Deprived of sleep one day, the body requires more the next day. But we need to start *educating* people instead of giving them drugs. Insomnia can be greatly helped, even eliminated, by changing the way we think.

By using your self-relaxation techniques this will be the start of helping to change your sleep patterns. Just think how good you will feel waking up in the morning feeling refreshed, re-energised and fully wide awake, ready for the day ahead. When did you last feel like that?

Isn't it time to start?

Now that you have made a commitment to 'change', this is the start of a whole new life. Your sleep patterns will improve, you will sleep better, feel better and look better. You'll feel more in control of your life. Do you want to know my Butterfly Prescription for Health?

It is VITAL that we think POSITIVE THOUGHTS.
It is VITAL that we use POSITIVE WORDS.
It is VITAL that we ACT POSITIVELY

The Butterfly Experience Health Plan

By using *The Butterfly Experience* Health Plan, you are taking the first important steps to creating a new healthy you. Caterpillars have weak sight – I want to help you see how important this area of your life is.

1. If you are worried or anxious about any part of your body please consult your doctor for advice.

2. Make sure your doctor refers you to an appropriate consultant or specialist. (If you are really concerned it may be appropriate for you to get treatment privately).

3. Find out as much as you can about your condition and the various treatments that are available. Your body already knows how to heal itself. As soon as treatment starts your own body goes into action to heal itself naturally.

4. It may be that you need to start changing your diet and looking at your lifestyle. Change your way of thinking to a more positive mindset. *You Can Heal Your Life* by Louise L Hay is an excellent book that will get you thinking about your life. It will help you begin the process of clearing out your negative thinking and help you to start loving yourself more in life.

5. Realise that having a positive mindset will help you to heal

more quickly.

6. Use *The Butterfly Experience* self-relaxation techniques. I know no more powerful treatment.

7. Have an open mind. Be willing to change if necessary. Look to the future in a positive way. It is time for you to accept and heal. Few people are aware of how their life-view, their *thought* life, has impacted on them physically. How is your thinking affecting your health?

8. Remembering that you are treating the mind, body and spirit, helping each aspect to feel healthier.

9. Accept help.

10. Stop only pleasing others. Make yourself number one.

At the end of its life stage, the caterpillar seeks out a safe place where it will evolve again, entering into the third stage of its metamorphosis. Using a silken girdle it attaches itself safely to this chosen place and encases itself in a chrysalis.

The chrysalis can turn a beautiful bronze or golden colour, as if in celebration of the wonders that are about to take place. Can you feel it happening?

You think this is good? Wait till the next stage!

15

Cocooning

The Cocoon is where the miracle happens – it's a mysterious, fascinating facet of *The Butterfly Experience*. In it we stop our wanderings and rest in our quest – we take stock. We look to the future, to the 'reveal', where we emerge as the miracle we're supposed to be. In the cocoon stage we go within. We strengthen and prepare ourselves for the next stage of our transformation. This is where we change from being a bizarre, ugly, defensive caterpillar and become our authentic selves.

Far from being a dormant stage, an amazing mini metamorphosis is taking place within the cocoon. Each stage creates fabulous patterns and colours which will differentiate us from others. There is 'inner movement' as the changes take place. A butterfly's wings have to be strong before it can fly. Inside the cocoon it makes tiny movements, building up its strength. If the cocoon were to be split prematurely, the butterfly would die.

Let's recap. In the first stage you've come to know yourself better. You've learned to recognise what's holding you back. Stage two helped you identify and remove what was holding you back. It gave you an energy boost for the important work ahead. The Cocoon takes these ideas a step further and asks you to go even deeper within, asking you the important questions that heal, so you can go on and live a magnificent life. I want to show you how to build on and develop seven vital qualities that maximise *The Butterfly Experience*. As you read through the next section ask yourself, 'Do I have these qualities in good measure?' Be honest - what do you still have to work on?

The seven 'must haves' for the Cocoon are: DESIRE, SELF-BELIEF, PERSEVERANCE, TRUST, DETERMINATION, SELF-DISCIPLINE AND GRATITUDE.

DESIRE

*'What things so ever ye desire, when ye pray,
believe that ye receive them, and ye shall have them'*
(Mark xi, 24)

Nowadays it would be easy to feel qualifications are a must-have to enable one to get on in life. But what if you don't have those exam results in your pocket? If *that's* been your excuse up till now, it's time to think again. Did you know that many of our top business people don't have degrees?

Richard Branson is a maverick who has transformed the way business operates in this country. Richard left school at sixteen, having struggled with dyslexia. At the age of eighteen he had founded Virgin Records. By the age of twenty-four he had bought the Virgin Islands. His forward thinking includes everyone – that's how he spreads his success. He has achieved untold wealth. Yet despite being a multimillionaire, Richard still has a burning *desire* to be successful. He never takes that success for granted.

And he still has fire in his belly. Far from kicking back and living the good life, he's an advocate for the environment. He also pays his staff handsome bonuses as a thank you for their hard work.

Let me give you another example. Back at the beginning of last century, Henry Ford was a man with no qualifications from an extremely poor background. His *desire* was to create a horseless carriage. Ford, like Branson, was prepared to do things differently. He made changes to the way cars had been manufactured till then. He paid his staff high wages and had a global vision for the wealth he created.

Most of his fortune was left to the Ford Foundation, which encourages education all around the world. We all have a deep, burning *desire* for success. We all need and want to be recognised for our contribution, for our unique talents. Not everyone's talents are best suited to the world of business. Sometimes it's hard to admit even to ourselves that we don't want to follow a conventional path. There's a lot of pressure from parents, teachers and friends to take the established route to 'success'. But is it right for you?

Ask yourself – what do I truly consider success to be? If we're on the path that's wrong for us, even though we become successful, it may well feel hollow. Happiness for ourselves may not be what others would have hoped for us. Success is different for everyone. For me success means simply being the best you can be. Turn to your journal and write what you consider success to be. Write down all the things that you think make people successful and also write down what would make *you* feel successful. Trust your instinct. Don't judge yourself in the process. Something you write down, it may be the tenth or the twentieth thing, will jump out at you and give you another piece of your jigsaw.

My own *desire* has always been to help others. Over the years it became so strong that, after qualifying in Clinical Hypnosis, I decided to open my own Clinic. Investing my own money I started out as a single practitioner. Running a home, looking after three children and furthering my training in the evenings, without the burning *desire* to make a success of my new business I might have given up. *Desire* is the best motivator I know – the hard work soon began to pay off. Before long I had several therapists working for me and was owner/operator of one of the largest complementary health Clinics in Glasgow. *Desire* starts inside us; that's where the magic is. It's always there, buoying us up when things backfire. It's what tells us to keep on going even when we get a knock back. *Desire* insists we find alternatives, reminds us that setbacks just make us stronger. *Desire* is what fuels our perseverance; it's the fire in our bellies that makes us go on.

> *'Yesterday is gone. Tomorrow has not yet come.*
> *We have only today. Let us begin'*
>
> Mother Teresa

Reading autobiographies of people I admire gives me a sense of their *desire*. Frank Bruno wanted to be the Heavyweight Champion of the World. His book describes how he was beaten on three previous attempts until he learned his lesson - that he had to work harder. Frank's *desire* to become world champion was so powerful it was 'like a drug'. That's a great analogy – and that's how badly you have to want it. Your

105

desire has to be strong enough to keep you going when times are hard. On his *fourth attempt,* Frank's desire paid off. He won.

The *desire* to succeed requires a certain quality – it has to be 100%. When you truly *believe* you can achieve your *desire* things automatically begin to happen. I never, ever give in. Which is not to say I've not met difficulties along the way. But my *desire* to succeed withstood any knock back. I never use the word 'failure'. I don't believe in it. I believe in learning from my mistakes. I believe in using *desire* to push past boundaries, to take me out of my comfort zone to where I can achieve success. And you can do it too.

To achieve our true *desires* we must first make them real. And then we have to invest energy in it. Successful people act on their desires. They set a plan and see it through. Nothing stops them. Don't just be a dreamer.

'Success usually comes to those
who are too busy to be looking for it'
Henry David Thoreau

A word of warning. Many people have achieved success, only to find that their business crashes and they lose everything – house, marriage, friendships. Their *desire* to achieve made them successful but they lost focus on what was really important in life. Not material things, but values and standards.

SELF-BELIEF

'I knew I was going to be a comedian when I was six.
You get what you believe you'll get.
You have to really want it and you'll get it'
Billy Connelly

Our DNA identifies us uniquely, like our fingerprints. I believe our *self-belief* does that too. *Self-Belief* is imperative. With it we can overcome any challenge. We must absolutely rid our minds of negative thoughts. If we don't believe in ourselves then how can we expect others to believe in us?

106

When we have *self-belief* we give off a positive energy. Our attitude is contagious. We approach tasks in a more positive way. How often have you heard stars or musicians interviewed who say they just *knew* that it was going to happen for them? They believed it so much they actually created their own opportunity. Regardless of the opinions of others, they believed anything was possible. Believing in ourselves starts in our hearts. That's where the magic is.

Darius Danesh is a great example of *self-belief*. Millions of people witnessed him being sent home by the Pop Star judges. But Darius has *desire*. He has *self-belief*. And he has *determination*. Instead of licking his wounds, he decided to reinvent himself. He changed his image, worked on new material and applied for *Pop Idol*. His determination to make it was so strong, he simply wasn't prepared to give up. When he was told that he was not pop star material, Darius' response was, 'I'll have a Number One hit and a platinum record by the time I'm thirty five.' He achieved it too, through sheer determination. Not only has he achieved worldwide critical success for his song writing, but he's the youngest male artist ever invited to play the lead role in Chicago. I had the privilege of watching him onstage. He's a true artist.

Do you believe in yourself? Do you truly believe you can achieve what you set out to? If the answer to those questions wasn't a resounding 'Yes!' don't give up hope. All beliefs are learned beliefs. Our *self-belief* is shaped in the cradle of our families. Our environment shapes the way we feel about ourselves.

Sometimes children are conditioned to believe they're not as good as siblings or friends. This is simply not true. We are all different, with unique gifts. Any negative beliefs you have about yourself can be altered. This process is already underway within you. The previous two stages have identified any old beliefs which were harming you. Now you have to be clear what your *new* beliefs about yourself are.

In order to do this we use the technique visualisation, which I'll teach you later in the chapter. Using it you'll learn to eradicate old, damaging ideas. Visualisation will allow you to see your best self. It well let you imagine enjoying what you really want. When you really believe good things are possible – a pay rise, a better relationship with your boss, greater opportunities to show what you can do - your behaviour starts to change. Your attitude changes. You look and sound more confident.

Confidence is a by-product of increased *self-belief*. Almost like a chain reaction, visualisation brings the necessary change.

> *'You have got to find success on your own terms –*
> *don't imitate others'*
>
> Harrison Ford

When you start to believe in *who* you are, not *what* you are, life becomes abundant – and that abundance comes in many guises. A strong *desire* and real *self-belief* – these factors alone can help people achieve the impossible. The spiritual axiom 'To thine own self be true' is paramount. We can't afford to compromise who we are. Be yourself. When we act badly or think negatively we transmit that to others subconsciously. Gossiping, backstabbing, laziness – none of these have any place in a positive life. When you feel good about yourself you radiate positive energy. And that makes you attractive to others.

I've experienced it in my own life. I always believed in myself. Through my own desire, self-belief, perseverance, trust, determination, self-discipline and gratitude this book was written. I never gave up on my dream of sharing my vision, of helping to change the world. And I always knew this book would be a best seller!

PERSEVERANCE

Combine *perseverance* with the other ingredients for success and life gives us rewards. I believe that each and every one of us has the determination to achieve. We just need the right motivation and then we have to dig deep.

We have so many positive examples of this quality in history, but one of my favourites is the Winston Churchill quote: *'Never give in – never, never, never give in'*. Churchill led a nation to victory!

We don't have to look far for other amazing stories of *perseverance*. Nelson Mandela was imprisoned for *twenty-seven* years. Determined to tell the world his country's story, he kept himself motivated every day using positive statements. He never gave up believing that he would see his country free of apartheid. Even from his prison cell he never stopped working towards his goal.

How badly do you want your dream? How determined are you to achieve success? Perseverance makes you pick yourself up when you're down. There are times when I feel below par, but I know that no one can pick me up but myself. I always seem to find an inner strength and the determination to go on – because I go looking for it!

We don't get good at anything unless we practice. That's exactly what you have to do with the Butterfly Techniques. Remember that you brought years of negative thinking to this Experience. You can't expect the people around you to change overnight. It has to start with you. PRACTICE! PRACTICE! PRACTICE!

'Nothing in the world can take the place of persistence'
Calvin Coolidge

You're learning how to become a new you with new thoughts, new ideas. You don't need to wait until you get to the end of the book before making changes. You can decide right here, right now that this is the beginning of something wonderful. If something feels right, have the courage to do what's needed. NO restrictions. Change is scary but so is staying stagnant. Don't deprive yourself. Make full use of the opportunity provided in *The Butterfly Experience*.

'A person should set his goals as early as he can and devote all his energy and talent to getting there. With enough effort, he may achieve it. Or he may find something that is even more rewarding. But in the end, no matter what the outcome, he will know he has been alive'
Walt Disney

Walt Disney was sitting with his two daughters in a local park when he had a vision. In it he saw people from all over the world, children and adults alike, having the time of their lives in a wonderful fun park. From this same vision came Snow White. As he sat thinking about his dream, he began to wonder how he could achieve his goal. Where could the park be? What would it cost? How would he convince banks to fund it?

We all have ideas. We all daydream. What made Disney different? He *never gave up*. Even after *three hundred and two* banks refused him funding for his project, he kept on going. It took years of hard work, raising finance, dealing with disappointments, but Disney *stayed focused on his goal*. Ten years on, by 1965, fifty million people had gone through the gates of Disneyland.

Like Disney we need a feeling of adventure when we set out our goals, a fantasy in our head. We need a frontier spirit as we head for our Tomorrowland. Disney teaches us another vital lesson – the power of the imagination. No matter what age we are, our inner child still yearns for fun and laughter, for adventure. Good goal setting includes all these things. Imagination is one of the most important tools available to us. Children are fantastic because they allow their imagination free rein. They don't judge or limit themselves. Let your head run wild. Think of all the wonderful, positive things you want to achieve in your life, the places you want to see, the people you want to meet, the things you want to accomplish, the people you would like to help.

Too many people nowadays want everything handed to them without working for it. If you don't get a promotion, do you walk away? If a business fails, are you prepared to start all over again? Or are you prepared to learn from your experience?

Perseverance will get you what you want. 90% of people in life are less successful than they should be because they fall at the first hurdle. It is only the 'stubborn' 10% with grit who learn the lessons they need to. Those lessons make our belief stronger.

'We haven't failed. We now know a thousand things that won't work, so we're that much closer to finding what will'

Thomas Edison

TRUST

'Having chosen our course, without guile and with pure purpose, let us renew our trust in God, and go forward without fear and with manly hearts'

Abraham Lincoln

110

Trust is a very small word but has a huge impact on our lives. If we cannot *trust* ourselves then how can we expect anyone to *trust* us? We have discovered what our desires are. Now we have to build on our belief in ourselves and *trust* the process of life. This is extremely hard – we fear the loss of control. We have to work on trust each and every day for the rest of our lives. But it's the answer to our fears.

Without *trust* in a Greater Reality we are reliant on ourselves. And we know how easily we make mistakes. God is our Provider. When we put our *trust* in Spirit to the test, especially when life is it's most painful, we trust that He will see us through. St. Peter's trust wavered when Jesus stretched out his hand to him and commanded that he walk across the angry waters. He was asking for his trust (Mathew 15: 22-33). This story tells us that we need to trust in God absolutely. We have to believe He will supply whatever it is that we need. We only have to ask. For years I sought proof – but I've learned over the years that trusting brings miracles. And you can't explain them – otherwise they wouldn't be miracles.

We have to trust to the process of life. We trust our doctors and medical profession when we need their help. We put our lives in their hands and *trust* that all will be well. We *trust* our friends, colleagues and family. We know they'll be there for us in times of need. *Trust* is a very powerful, very intimate act.

Trust is a vital ingredient in a happy life. It is vital in others – we should surround ourselves only with people with whom we feel instinctively secure. Above all we have to be trustworthy. We have to be genuine, discreet. We have to follow through on our promises if we are to find the sort of friendship which truly sustains us. Being a trustworthy person, acting honourably, living according to spiritual principles all times – these things also change how we feel about ourselves.

Learning to trust takes courage. Even if you've been hurt in the past, don't allow past events to stop you experiencing happiness today. It doesn't have to be a revolutionary change in character, an overnight thing. Remember the cocoon, all those tiny movements that one day will bring release.

'Men of genius are admired, men of wealth are envied, men of power are feared; but only men of character are trusted'
Alfred Adler

DETERMINATION

'Determination is the wake-up call to the human will'
Anthony Robbins

Benjamin Franklin is an example of a man who became successful because he mastered the art of *determination*. He tried over five thousand times before he was able to make the first light bulb. Every time the experiment failed he looked to see what he could learn from it. It would have been tempting to give up after the first thousand or two thousand times, don't you think? But winners never quit, and quitters never win. I never take no for an answer. No matter what the task I will find a way to make it work and I'll keep going until it does. It's in my blood, my DNA.

You only get back in life what you give out. If I keep on striving to be the best, someone turns up to help me. It's that trust thing again. You have to believe it will happen.

Here in Scotland Tom Hunter made his mark and his fortune in commerce. Tom is someone I greatly admire for his *determination*. He's been knighted for his vision as an entrepreneur and his philanthropy. Did you know Tom began his career selling trainers out of the back of a van? Life hasn't always been easy for him – even after he made his money. His motivation has always been to help educate young children. He recently donated a million pounds to the Children In Need appeal. One of the wealthiest people in the world today, Tom understands the need to pass on what he has been given. His Hunter Foundation is inspirational. But Tom's attitude of *never give up* inspires me more.

Determination builds character. It makes us a better person. It helps us prioritise, maximise our time for positive results. *Determination* is a tool – it lets us win in spite of our limitations. *Determination*

112

gets us out of trouble. *Determination* is what helps us to improve our relationships and achieve great things.

'The price of success is hard work, dedication to the job at hand, and the determination that whether we win or lose, we have applied the best of ourselves to the task at hand'

Vince Lombardi

SELF-DISCIPLINE

'If you put off everything till you're sure of it, you'll get nothing done'

Norman Vincent Peale

Lack of self-discipline is a common source of low self-esteem. How many times have you told yourself, 'I wish I had more will power!'? How many times have you started to do something, only to give up at the first hurdle? We've all had experiences like these. Say you want to stop smoking. You start the day off telling yourself you're going to stop. But by lunch time you are having a cigarette. Why? You need more self-discipline.

What is self-discipline? Self-discipline is doing what needs to be done, regardless of how you're feeling. Self-discipline shreds problems. It stops us procrastinating, it makes our lives more orderly, it allows us to solve problems *today*. Combined with the goal setting ideas I'm going to teach you later in this chapter, it is a powerful tool.

People make the mistake of thinking just because they fail to follow through on something big that they should give up entirely. Self-discipline is like spiritual muscle – the more you use it the stronger it becomes. The paradox is it takes self-discipline to become more self-disciplined. So set yourself targets, small goals at first and follow through on them. Tidy those cupboards. Rewrite your phone directory that's falling apart. Make that phone call you've been putting off.

Every day give yourself simple tasks and at the end of the day tick them off in your journal. Then gradually increase the challenge. Telling someone you trust what you're doing will help – they can hold

113

you accountable.

Every day up the ante. Enjoy the benefits of a life of self-discipline and soon there will be no going back. Every time you succeed at something give yourself a small reward.

Self-discipline is a vital characteristic of success – because it helps us control our reactions. Now that you know how to temper your negative emotions and learn lessons from every situation, developing it is going to be so much easier. Affirm your new self-discipline to yourself daily.

'We all have dreams. But in order to make dreams into reality, it takes an awful lot of determination and self-discipline'
Jesse Owens

GRATITUDE

Do you sometimes think you're the only one the rain falls on? Catch yourself wondering what you did to deserve x, y, z? It's draining and time wasting. Use some of the self-discipline we were just talking about to start thinking in a more positive manner. When you find yourself thinking negatively, ask yourself - what have I learned from this experience? How could I have done things differently? Acknowledge the feelings and emotions that are being alerted to you. Move on by using the self-relaxation technique. Visualise the way you would have liked it to be, writing down your thoughts. The next time a similar situation arises, act on them.

Now let's look at what gratitude really means. It means being grateful for *all* the things in your life. Grab your journal. Write down all the things you are grateful for, e.g. your home, family, job, life, health, car, friends, food, pets, your ideas and opportunities.

Really think here what you are grateful for. If you're struggling, just think a moment about people who live hand to mouth in rented accommodation, waiting on a government subsidy. Think about the starving of the world. No running water, no food, no shelter.

How do you feel about your life now? You don't have to spend money to feel blessed. Gratitude is about your attitude to life. One

114

man sits in front of the telly, beer in hand, moaning about the state of the world. Another could sit in the same room enjoying the programme others have made for him and enjoying the company of his precious family.

Life is precious. And it can be short. It's so easy to forget that until something happens.

'Let us rise up and be thankful, for if we didn't learn a lot today, at least we learned a little, and if we didn't learn a little, at least we didn't get sick, and if we got sick, at least we didn't die; so, let us all be thankful'

Buddha

All of these character traits stem from a key concept we have to address in Cocoon. Self-respect. As we've worked through this book you've learned to be calmer, to focus your attention on what you want. Now it's time for one of the most important challenges *The Butterfly Experience* offers – changing your relationship with YOU.

If I asked you to name the most important relationship in your life, most of you would probably name your partner, your children or your parents. I'm asking you to consider another idea; that the most important relationship you will ever have in life is with *yourself*.

Our self image is vital for good self-esteem. It affects our personality, moulds our behaviour, colours our attitude. If it's good it helps our confidence. If it's poor, people are able to tell immediately. What we think about ourselves shapes who we are.

How is your self image? Do you wake up in the morning feeling fantastic? Do you feel good about yourself on the inside? Do you believe you are a fabulous, happy, healthy, sexy, gorgeous, loving, caring, compassionate, special human being? Or do those words make you cringe?

Why do we find it so difficult to accept the way we are? Ask yourself that question, then listen to the answer you receive. Listen to your body, what it's telling you - the more you balk at positive statements about yourself, the more you need to do this work!

Do you put yourself down? Do you let others put you down?

Without good self esteem our mood is dependent on the good graces of others – because we haven't learned to be happy in our own skin. Phil McGraw says,

'You have the power to be miserable the rest of your life. Or you can say, "I'm going to give myself the permission to heal." You have to decide whether you're going to define a new relationship with yourself and remove the roadblocks that are blocking your path to living your best life.'

Without a positive self-image it's impossible to have a full, loving relationship with anyone else. Negative thoughts about ourselves inevitably impact on those around us. Problems creep in, often repeating themselves time and time again - because we haven't yet learned our lessons. Do you constantly try and please others? Are you trying to be what you think others want you to be? Are you living your life to please your parents? Do you get butterflies every time you have to say no?

We learn from our elders. Their insecurities influence the way they rear or mentor us. As a result we sometimes grow up believing we're not good enough. Acknowledging that helps. But sometimes we get stuck in a rut of blaming others, rather than moving on. Is that true of you?

Is there resentment in your life that's holding you back? How long are you prepared to blame the past for the way your life is today? Yes, we were conditioned as children, but every new day is a chance to refocus, rethink, recharge. You're an adult now – you choose the direction your life takes.

A new relationship with yourself is the true start of your new life. It's important that you understand this. Every relationship we have moves to a new level – as soon as we drop the idea that we can find happiness in another person. All other relationships stem from our sense of self. Friendships blossom as you come to love and appreciate yourself. Dealings with colleagues ease. Sibling rivalries fade.

Your changed perspective allows others to be who they are. Romance deepens because you're willing your partner to grow with you. Love for your children becomes a free channel unblocked by false expectations.

So, what kind of relationship do you have with your mind? Your body? Your spirit? Frightened to find out? What if I told you everyone else knows how you feel about yourself just by looking at you! When we have low self-esteem it shows. Lacking confidence means we hold our body in a certain manner – shoulders rounded, body language defensive. It shows in our dress. It shows in our eye-contact, or the lack of it. Inability to meet someone's gaze means we have emotional pain. I'm going to work with you now on a technique to help you address that pain.

16

Mirror Work

Mirror work helps us face up to the truth about ourselves. There are two types of mirror work. First of all, let's talk about our bodies. Do you like every inch of your body? Do you like your face, even when you are tired and look a little puffy in the morning?

You have to love yourself no matter what you look like. You have to appreciate your body even when you're not well, when your energy is low. What's stopping you from feeling good about yourself, accepting yourself exactly the way you are? What's stopping you is comparing yourself to others!

We see horror pictures every day of famous women with anorexia or bulimia, tortured souls trying to live up to some false idea of what the world considers beautiful. The media has bombarded us with images of skeletal young women we're supposed to think are the norm. People go to extreme lengths to resemble those idealised images, for example: false breasts, hair extensions, liposuction, cheek enhancements etc. Where will it end? And what are the long-term effects? No one undergoes surgery like that unless they have a fundamental problem with body image. Look at the terrible results some unfortunates have - misshapen features, tumerous lips. Why take the risk?

It's not just women who sabotage their bodies. Men are competing with airbrushed photographs of genetically blessed young men who have a team of people working to keep them in optimum health.

They pump their bodies with steroids, use weights until they're bulging with muscles. They've become addicted to the idea of the perfect body shape. When will the world wake up to that fact that we're all individual? When will we start accepting our diversity and loving who we are, not how we look? Your genetic composition is yours alone. *Be proud of that.* It's time to celebrate our uniqueness.

When was the last time you looked at yourself naked? Really looked, not just long enough to pull a face at what you don't like. HAVE A GOOD LOOK AT YOURSELF IN THE MIRROR TODAY. WHAT DO YOU SEE?

We are all spirit beings in a physical body. Ask your body how it feels today. Can you feel self-doubt? Uncertainty? Keep working through it – I guarantee you that this technique will very quickly teach you to move forward in a gentle and loving way. Beauty on the outside is linked with the beauty that lies deep inside us. It is a reflection of a happy spirit. What we wear on the outside is a reflection of how we feel about ourselves inside. Do you feel good about yourself, take care of yourself? Do you exercise in a way you enjoy? Or do you cover up your body with baggy clothes?

There are people who are almost professional shoppers, thinking if they buy new clothes then they will feel better. Yes, that's true, for all of five minutes. But if you don't feel good on the inside then no amount of clothes will change the way you feel.

Do you take joy in your appearance or could you not care less how you look?

When I look in the mirror I see a gorgeous, wonderful, caring, compassionate woman. I truly love myself for who I am and what I stand for. Can you say that about yourself? We cannot buy happiness nor make it. Happiness comes from within.

Love it or hate it, your body is with you for life, unless you change your body with plastic surgery and even then you are only changing the outside, you are still you on the inside. It will carry you on your journey no matter where you go. Take a few moments to just think about how much your body has endured so far.

We should thank it every day for the hard work it does. Your body never gave up on you, no matter how hard you punished it. Look at your body as the body of someone who deserves to be happy. Who deserves to lead an abundant life. Your body needs to be looked after, cared for. It needs exercise to keep it healthy. To help you make good decisions about your body, let's first look inside *you*.

It's time for the next stage of our mirror work. The cocoon stage is amazing. It allows the caterpillar to completely disassemble. Every cell then moves to a predetermined place where they reassemble themselves in the cocoon into the shape of a butterfly. A new form, capable of flight. Close mirror work will get you there.

So many of us feel anger at ourselves. Deep down we *know* we've been complicit in things that have gone wrong. We're angry at ourselves for not standing up for what was right. Angry that we didn't do or say what was needed. We've allowed little grievances to stockpile until they become a great weight that threatens us.

We resent others, but most of all we resent ourselves. Removing that 'resentment of self' is an inside job that takes time. We have to deconstruct the walls we've built to protect our ego. But that's OK. There's no need to rush. This feeling has taken a lifetime to build up. It would be unrealistic to expect it to disappear quickly. It would be irresponsible of me not to include a warning here. Mirror work is extremely powerful. What we see in the mirror is actually a reflection of our inner self. The real you. Some people initially find the experience unsettling or even disturbing.

Mirror work helps us find out who we really are. Through it we overcome anger and resentment. We come to love ourselves. When we look in the mirror, deeply, not superficially, the way we feel about our Self changes. Why? Because by looking at yourself, *really* looking at yourself in the mirror, you start to see your Inner Child. You come to know that little boy or girl who is still there, deep inside you, who needs nurturing. Recognising it, you immediately understand the importance of taking care of the child within. It never goes away. Would you be unkind to your own daughter or son? Then why be unkind to your own inner child?

The kindest thing you can do for your inner child is release the emotions weighing it down. We have to free ourselves in order to move on. Let's get started.

This Butterfly Exercise requires forethought. You need space and time, uninterrupted time. Take the phone off the hook. Sit quietly and comfortably. When you are ready, look into a hand mirror.

Now, look at yourself. Who do you see? How do you feel? Do you feel silly? Do you feel embarrassed? Do you think 'This won't work'? or 'Do I have time for this?'

All these thoughts will be going around your head. That's perfectly natural. Look again. LOOK! I MEAN *REALLY* LOOK.

See that little girl or boy. Watch them looking back at you. That little girl or boy inside you, asking you not to hurt yourself any more. Look into their eyes. What do you want to say to them? And what are they trying to say to you?

Sometimes tears come up. That's perfectly acceptable. The tears show that you are feeling vulnerable. You are human and have feelings. Sometimes we've told ourselves so often that we're strong, that it hurts to see the tired, frightened child staring back at us.

LOOK AT YOURSELF AGAIN. SAY THREE POSITIVE BUTTERFLY AFFIRMATIONS TO YOUR INNER CHILD. For example:

- I am Healthy, Strong And Loving.
- I am Fabulous, Confident And Wise.
- I am Happy, Loving And Kind.

You decide what your three positive statements are.

Now I want you to close your eyes and imagine the person you *want* to be. Be specific. Go into great detail as you fantasise about that person.

How you would feel if you were that person? What would you look like? What would you dress like? What would your behaviour tell others? What would your career be? What would others say about you?

Imagine how the IDEAL YOU would feel and look. Open your eyes. Look in the mirror again. Repeat your three positive statements. *NOW* HOW DO YOU FEEL?

This technique is a vital part of changing your thought patterns to a positive mindset. Practice this technique every day for fifteen minutes. Do this for thirty days. Give yourself a tick in your journal or on your calendar each day. Give yourself a smiley face. If you forget to practice your mirror work, go back to the start of thirty days again. Your mind will soon train you to remember.

By repeating self-affirming statements every day you'll be

reinforcing a positive mindset and boosting your self-esteem. Your attitude to yourself will change. You will feel more vibrant and uplifted. Within *days* your friends will start to see a difference.

Below I have listed examples of positive Butterfly Affirmations suitable for close mirror work. You can choose some of them. But why not make up your own?

- I love myself exactly as I am
- I am strong, healthy and confident
- I am open to change
- My body radiates love
- Change is just another challenge
- I deserve the best, nothing but the best
- I attract all the abundance in the world
- I give of myself to others

The Man Who Thinks He Can

If you think you're beaten, you are
If you think you dare not, you don't
If you like to win but think you can't,
It's almost a synch you won't.
If you think you'll lose, your lost
For out in the world we find
Success begins with a fellow's will
It's all in a state of mind.
If you think your out-classed you are
You got to think high to rise
You got to be sure of yourself
Before you'll ever win the prize.
Life's battles don't always go
to the stronger or faster man
but soon or late the man who wins
Is the one who thinks he can!

Rudyard Kipling

We owe it to ourselves to treat ourselves with respect, kindness, dignity and love. Every day we grow another day older. Don't waste your time on earth. Every day when you wake up, tell your inner child how happy and loved you are.

Reinforce your new self-belief constantly. Things don't have to be perfect, as long as we are moving forward. How quickly do you want change to happen? Tick off those days and see the difference!

17

Visualisation

Here's another fabulous butterfly technique to help you maximise this time of Cocooning. Again, it's a technique I want you to use every day. It's called *Visualisation*.

Visualisation is a powerful way to manifest your dreams and desires that won't cost you any money. It may even manifest money for you! Sounds too good to be true?

Most people try to manifest their desires through sheer hard work. But that takes a lot of energy. Most of us don't achieve all our goals that way because we don't use the full capacity of our minds. We keep chasing our desires as they get further and further away. We all admire pop stars and actors who have made their dreams come true. How do you think they got to where they are? They had to believe in themselves. What makes them different is the *quality* of their self-belief and their ability to think BIG. They had to know what they wanted.

We don't realise how powerful our minds are until we start using this technique. By using visualisation we can manifest anything we want. I'm living proof that by using your thought process you can have *anything*. Today you have the chance to manifest anything you want through your thought processes, instead of chasing it all your life.

Visualisation works according to the Law of Attraction. By using this powerful tool you will be more in control of your life, you will be happier. Your success is guaranteed.

A childlike imagination is one of the most powerful resources available to us. If used well our lives are enhanced immeasurably by it. Remember a time when you wanted something really, really badly? Think of the effort and action you put into getting it. Think how positive you were about manifesting that item in your life, how you dreamed about it, seeing yourself with it. Think how it felt when you finally got it. Remember the euphoria?

Now think of the all times you *didn't believe* you would get something you wanted. What happened? And how did that feel? With visualisation you never need to feel that way again! I've used it to help manifest my own dreams. It will help you create an abundant life.

What is visualisation? Time for some learning by doing! Close your eyes. Use your imagination to put yourself into a picture. It's that simple. For example, think of the sun. Feel its warmth on your skin.

Turn the heat up. See its colour. Allow its heat to melt down through your body, gently healing it from head to toe. If you have trouble doing this the first time, remember it's like all the other practices in the book. Keep on doing it. If you practice often you'll start to feel it, generate it. The mind is truly amazing. Remember you are in control at all times.

In Cocoon, after using the self-relaxation technique, we build on our positive mindsets by using this new practice. How do we do it? By going within. The key to the kingdom, the secret, is in you.

Now you understand how to use your imagination, let's apply visualisation to your life. First free your mind of any mental clutter. Clear the debris that has gathered there. Allow your eyes to CLOSE comfortably.

Start to visualise any situation you would like to change. See the situation the way it is now. Now take one aspect of this situation and *change* it. Turn it into something positive. Here's a simple example. Your car is broken and you can't afford to pay to have it fixed. You would use visualisation by seeing yourself sitting in your car, driving around. At this stage you don't need to know how the car is going to be repaired. You just have to start *believing* it has already been fixed. Each time you do this visualisation, change the picture a little more. Focus.

Make the image in your head exactly as you want it to be. It may take some time. That's okay. Don't leave out any details.

Again, you need to believe in what you are doing, really believe it with all your heart. See the car fixed and yourself driving in it. No matter what, keep focusing on that picture. Let the picture be as colourful and as real as possible. Stay open to Spirit. Remember, the sub-conscious doesn't know what's true or untrue. Believe it will happen and then wait for the magic. First we manifest in our minds, then the wonder happens. Before long, help will be on its way. Before you know it you'll meet a friend who knows a mechanic who owes her a favour. You'll repay him by doing him a good turn. And so the cycle continues.

Practice visualisation every day. Remember, first find your inner calm. This calm helps us set our goals in a more directed way. Just by sitting quietly and visualising an outcome we are taking steps towards achieving our goals. Your imagination is powerful. Use it – visualise the changes you want to experience.

Meditate on your goal. Some inspiration, thought or piece of information will jump out. This is your unconscious talking to you. Trust your intuition. Thank it for its gift.

Now feel what it would be like to have *already achieved* your goal. What would that look like? How would it feel? What would it manifest in your life? Make those ideas as real as possible as you continue to visualise your life improving.

Now, make a renewed commitment to those goals. Write them down. Don't worry about how and when they are going to happen. You just need to believe that they will.

Is there any point going for an interview if you think you only *might* get the job? You have to believe that you *will* get the job. You have to smell, touch and *feel* the job. You have to see yourself in the position, doing the work well, enjoying it.

With visualisation you will start to believe that you have the job in the bag. When you go along for the interview you'll act as if you have the job. That self-belief comes across.

Never underestimate the power of visualisation. I've used it my whole life. I've waited for Cocoon to teach you this wonderful technique because I know that by now your thinking has changed. We visualise because we feel deep down inside that we deserve good things. At the same time visualisation promotes self-belief.

Warning. Your picture must be exactly as you want it to be. Remember the old saying 'be careful what you wish for'? Send out your wishes in specific form. Ask for what you want exactly.

Anne's Story

Anne came to see me, lacking in confidence. She blushed easily and was embarrassed because of it. When she arrived her body language oozed shyness. She wanted to share her life with someone, to start afresh. How could she ever meet someone new, feeling as she did? In our sessions it emerged that Anne's father had been unable to show affection. She had grown up craving more love.

I taught Anne how to 'create' the man of her dreams. Using visualisation, Anne was able to 'see' him, his height, his eyes, the colour of his hair. Anne included daily visualisation of her ideal partner in her morning routine and sent her wish out to the universe. As her confidence grew, her life opened up in other ways. On her third visit Anne looked fantastic. She glowed, saying she felt confident and really happy. Her body language was confident and there was no more blushing.

Anne had finally started to accept *who* she was. She chose to let go the feelings that were hurting her. Her father was living his life. It was Anne who was holding herself back. Anne is a wonderful example of how positive thinking can be introduced into your life and impact every part of it for the better.

Is it any wonder she had found a new partner to share her happiness with? The magic starts inside, way deep down. Anything can happen if you let it. Why not let the magic happen to your life? You deserve it. YOU ARE SPECIAL. I've asked you to use visualisation in the section that follows.

18

Seven Days to a Healthier Relationship with Yourself

Day One - Enhancing Visualisation

Make a promise to yourself now to ensure good, quality sleep for yourself. Establish a gentle unwinding routine that will tell your body you want it to sleep soon. Make sure your bed linens are fresh, that your bedroom is a sanctuary – calm and uncluttered. Go to bed at the same time every night, and rise at the same hour every morning.

You will soon have established a rhythm your body will come to expect. It's important to get plenty of sleep and rest so the body can recharge itself during the night and be rested for a new day. Unless we allow our body sufficient rest it will come to show signs of tiredness, and be lacking in energy. You will experience lethargy and suffer a poor appetite.

Wayne Dyer quotes a wonderful phrase from the poet Rumi, *'The morning breezes have secrets to tell you'*. For years now I've awoken each morning at the same time - 5.00am. I awake by my own *head clock,* which I set each night, trusting I will awaken at that time. Life is too precious to waste lying in bed.

I begin every day by doing self-relaxation and journaling. This is my spiritual discipline and I am faithful to it. This is my time, the time before the rest of the world wakes up. It's the best time of the day, still and peaceful. I can give my body and mind the time they need. I spend quiet moments feeding myself the right positive thoughts and giving my body healing. This is when I re-energise, refocus and ground myself for the day ahead.

Discipline is also an important part of the *visualisation* techniques I use. I daily reinforce in my mind how I want the day to unfold, planning events and meetings ahead as though they had actually taken place. I make sure to incorporate the things I want to happen, enjoying the positive outcomes I see. Then I give myself three positive affirmations for the day. These are designed to keep me focused and energised for the day ahead.

I dance to wake up and energise my body – usually to the Celine Dion anthem, 'I'm Alive'. As I dance I celebrate my life, awakening the spirit within me. The physical movement gets the blood circulating round my body. My gratitude helps me to feel bright and awake. Dancing - or any form of exercise such as yoga or tai chi - raises my vibrations and helps me begin the day with a good level of energy. Without it I would struggle to cope with problems that might arise. I need lots of energy to deal with patients' problems and motivate them.

Finally I look in the mirror, telling myself that I am strong, healthy and wonderful. I'm now ready for the day ahead.

Day Two - Sharpening Hearing

Today let's focus on *hearing*. I work constantly on heightening my hearing awareness. Paradoxically I do this by becoming aware of the stillness around me. So few people ever simply sit in silence and just listen. It's a powerful, life-enhancing gift to us. We need silence so that we can listen to the answers our inner knowing will provide.

If this concept is new to you, you may struggle initially to sit in silence. Connection to Spirit is a two way channel – we talk to our Source. But we must also listen. The secret is to have no expectations, either of yourself or of the Power that is waiting for you to turn to it. Don't be disappointed if you're not immediately enlightened. Be patient. It will come.

Don't allow any distractions. If a thought attempts to intrude, simply acknowledge it, saying to yourself, 'Thinking'. If a noise distracts you, say to yourself, 'Hearing', and bring yourself back to your inner silence. If your nose starts to itch, don't scratch – the itch will only come back somewhere else. Acknowledge the itch – and let it pass.

When you are still and centred, breathing deeply and regularly, ask your Higher Self questions - how can you move on in life? Or we ask for a sign for ways to fulfil ourselves today. Or ask for people to be put in our path – people who will help us move on. Sometimes the questions are quite specific.

After spending time listening and being, I might practice visualisation again. Part of that is planning things I want to hear that day. I will imagine a situation – for example going along to the company I'm visiting. I hear the owners tell how happy they are with my work and asking me back.

Another way we can lift our spirits is through music. Throughout the day I listen to music that uplifts me. I have always made it part of my life. It changes how we feel. Music is a vibration. It can lift our mood or it can make us feel sad. When you go to a pop concert you can feel the energy rising in the hall. Everyone leaves uplifted even though they may have gone along feeling quite low. All their worries have left them. Now think of the music troubled teenagers listen to. Research has proven the link between dark, angry music and teenage suicide. Be careful about what you allow yourself to listen to.

Music should be used as a healing experience, or an energiser. It's played to patients in a coma state to help them awaken! Use this wonderful symptom-free antidote to life's ills as often as possible.

Don't accept others talking to you in a negative fashion. RED-X it out. Do not accept any negative words or phrases from anyone. But more importantly, make today the day you start using positive language to yourself and others.

Would you accept your friend telling you that you look fat and tired? Or that you have big ears and look terrible? Of course you wouldn't! Then why speak to yourself like that? When you talk to yourself in a positive way your body reacts.

Day Three - Heightening Our Sense Of Smell

While doing your self-relaxation today, heighten your sense of smell. Light a scented candle which will help you to relax as you begin your Morning Time. By thinking about the smells around us, in our food, perfume, flowers, fruit, we become more aware of them.

131

Today, spend time in the bath rather than in the shower. Soak in luxuriously scented water. Cleanse your body with a loofah or scrub brush, ridding your body of dead skin cells. Afterwards, massage yourself lovingly with oils using scented cream to nourish your body's surface. We don't have to spend lots of money to do it. A few drops of essential oils in base oil such as almond will suffice. The skin is the body's largest organ. Pamper it. It's great to look after yourself, taking care of your body.

Our inner child relishes the sense of touch and the scent calms or uplifts us as we require. Light a candle whose smell reminds you of childhood before you do your mirror work today. I remind myself I'm doing this work to help me accept myself as I am. I look at my inner child and ask her how I can improve her life. We can never give too much attention to our inner child. How can we help others if we don't help ourselves first?

Day Four - Improving Taste

Today we are focusing on new foods. My body has become very sensitive to certain foods - I have become intolerant to wheat. So many foods are made from wheat and my body has been communicating that to me over the last few years. I love trying new food sensations and eating healthily; I know that the nourishment I give my body raises my energy vibration. Eating well helps me to stay bright and alert. Eat slowly, relishing the different tastes on your tongue.

Make a healthy meal for the family. Spend quiet time. If you enjoy reading, indulge yourself. Treat yourself to a cake or some chocolate. It doesn't need to be your birthday for you to be kind to yourself. I always make time for myself in the day, even if it is only for a short while. No one else is going to look after you the way you know you need looking after.

What about food for our thoughts? Each of us has negative thoughts throughout the day. It's how we deal with them that makes the difference. By treating ourselves badly, we're also telling other people how to treat us, so it's a self-perpetuating cycle.

I always journal a gratitude list at the end of the day, to thank the universe for the wonderful moments I've experienced and all the abundance I've been given. I thank the universe for the food and shelter that have been mine, for the love in my family. We take such things for granted but there are so many people in life whose basic needs for comfort and security aren't met. You never know what's around the corner, so be appreciative of life's bounty.

Day Five - Touch Awareness

Starting my day with self-relaxation helps set me up for the day. It quietens my mind and helps me be more focused. I constantly need to work on myself if I'm going to be strong enough to help others. When you get up in the morning look in the mirror and tell yourself you are gorgeous, beautiful, strong, healthy and confident. Who else is going to tell you?

After showering I oil my body, massage my face, repeating the movements slowly and lovingly. By doing this I give my body the respect it deserves. My attitude to myself is different.

My self-relaxation helps me to be more aware of my body. I will start the day by talking to my body in a positive way. I will wear soft fabrics that caress it. Clothes speak volumes about how you feel about yourself. Do you wear baggy clothes to hide your shape? Do you wear dark fabrics all the time? Are you happy with your shape and comfortable in your own skin? Lying to ourselves about what size we are is foolish. Have you clothes in your wardrobe you haven't been able to wear for years but don't want to throw out because of the memories surrounding them? Or do you fear that if you throw them away you'll never get back to that size? So many women have a range of sizes in their wardrobe. Don't yo-yo diet. Why not experiment with brightly coloured, fitted clothes that show off your shape? Today I want you to accept who you are and the size you are and CLEAR OUT YOUR WARDROBE!

For fun and to heighten my sense of touch I enjoy spending time shuffling a pack of playing cards. I will look at the colours and the suits of the cards. I then close my eyes and feel the cards. I ask myself to tell me when I am touching a red card by making that colour bright in my mind. When I touch a black card I ask my mind to make it dull. This heightens my awareness. I am feeling the colours, seeing the images with my inner eye.

I make positive Butterfly Affirmation cards and plant them around my home in places where I can read them aloud to myself as the day passes. I feel happier and more in control. In order to change negative thinking, we first have to be aware of our thoughts.

Day Six - Energy Awareness

Today we're going to make a conscious effort to be kind to ourselves, to treat ourselves the way we would treat our own best friend. Declare Saturday your day (or choose the day that suits you best). Make it the day you celebrate who you are. Buy yourself a treat, a bouquet of flowers or a video. When was the last time you pampered yourself, bought yourself a bunch of flowers or had a game of golf with your friends? Why wait to be kind to yourself on your birthday? Tell yourself you love yourself, pamper yourself, treat yourself. You have to make yourself *feel* extra special and soon you'll start to believe it!

By doing our self-relaxation every day and raising our vibrations we have the energy required for our busy lives. But today I want you to focus on ways to bring your energy levels down. If you are feeling harassed or stressed, pamper yourself. Enjoy a long soak in the bath. I always take time each week to simply sit in my garden, or in a park for thirty minutes, listening to the birds and the wind talk. I heighten my awareness of the world around me - the plants are energy, the grass under my feet is energy. I ground myself in it, absorb it consciously. It is such a calming feeling. By breathing deeply and freely we can expand our energy vibration. This will help you to be more in control of your emotions.

Our belongings all have our energy in them and with practice we can all pick up on this. To keep my intuition attuned I attend a medium circle. But you don't have to belong to a group like mine to practice this. We only have to be open to using all our senses. Ask your friends to sit in a circle. Swap belongings, without knowing who they belong to. Touch them, picking up on their vibration. Close your eyes and ask your Higher Self for any information on that object. You will be surprised at how often your 'gut instinct' is right. Very quickly you will sense and feel the energy from the object. You may even see pictures in your mind's eye - trust your instincts.

Day Seven

After practicing your self-relaxation and raising your vibrations, spend time sending out positive energy to the world. Not to individuals, but to the universe, knowing your energy is contributing to make the world a better place. Spend time today researching, looking at a spiritual practice that will provide structure and discipline for your life.

Now that you have reached the end of the week, you are now on your way to looking and feeling better. You should be looking forward to spending a relaxing day doing whatever you want. Reading that book you've been looking forward to or going for a drive to a favourite spot that uplifts your spirit. Today is a do anything day. You choose.

I always make sure that at some point in the week I go for a brisk walk. Exercise stimulates the blood and helps it to pump around your body, as well as burning any fat. It keeps your body healthy and makes you feel invigorated. Walking is wonderful exercise and it doesn't cost anything but shoe leather. Exercise is healthy and counteracts depression, so make sure you incorporate it into your week, several times a week.

You can join a gym, but make sure you are doing something you enjoy, otherwise it'll be short-lived. Think of what you've always wanted to do - again, it has to be realistic, achievable. Join a hill-climbing group, a salsa class, learn to kayak – and remember the value of exercising with others. That's a great motivator. This is a day to do whatever you want and appreciate your life. Enjoy it. Recharge your batteries for a new week ahead.

If you're blessed with family, make a conscious decision to enjoy them. We spend so much time working and don't give enough time to our loved ones. MAKE THAT TIME NOW. MARK IT IN YOUR DIARY.

We all need support and unconditional acceptance. We find it and give it at home, but there will always be times in life when we need extra strength and extra support – from friends, our Spirit source, from our inner selves. It makes sense to top up our spiritual bank, often and generously – so that we have sufficient resources when times are harder.

You have the choice to step out of your comfort zone right NOW and start to live the life you've always dreamed of. An abundant life is not just for other people, it's for you too. You are part of this world, a part of God. All you have to do is make a decision to claim your birthright.

You may feel trapped still – the last vestiges of pride and fear may still be holding you back. Don't let old thinking get in the way of what you deserve. Sometimes in life we have to ask for help. If that's the way you're feeling, turn now to Spirit and ask for courage. That thought will be picked up as a vibration and help will come. In fact you're already attracting it by sending out the positive energy.

Young locusts are called hoppers. Do you hop around in life not knowing where you're going? When locusts become adults they only know how to fly in the one direction – the one the wind takes them in. They blindly use up all their resources and when those resources are all used up they die.

Now that you are more positive and feeling happier about yourself you can start to create abundance in your life your way. Don't just follow other people blindly. Why live as a locust when you could be a butterfly? That is your choice. Only you can make the changes in your life that will bring joy, happiness and abundance. Your tool bag is filled with goodies, already overflowing with abundance.

A little faith. A little courage. Can you feel that the cocoon is starting to open? I hope you feel a building sense of urgency and excitement. I want you to harness the energy you're feeling now to best purpose. I want to teach you the skill that will get you to where you want to be in life. I want to teach you...

19

The Importance Of Goals

*'All successful people have a goal. No one can get anywhere unless
he knows where he wants to go and what he wants to do'*
Norman Vincent Peale

Most people are afraid to set a goal. Goals take them too far out of
their comfort zone. They'd rather feel safe and secure in their old
patterns and routines. But goal setting is what sets successful people
apart from the herd. Goals mean being courageous. It means being
brave enough to set out all the things you want to achieve. When we
set goals we are raising our standards, giving ourselves a focus and
path to walk.

Setting your goal is as important as achieving it. Once you set your
goal, magical things begin to happen. You have sent your wish, your
thoughts and mental images out into the universe.

Speak your truth in life. Don't be afraid to tell people what your
dreams are.

*'Every time you state what you want or believe, you're the first to
hear it. It's a message to both you and others about what you think
are possible. Don't put a ceiling on yourself'*
Oprah Winfrey

Oprah uses her television programme as a vehicle for inspirational
people to tell their story. Oprah's own life was not always happy.
Sexually abused as a child, she comforted herself with food. But
Oprah had a goal - she wanted to help others. Overweight, a woman
and black, she had a hard road ahead of her, one that would have had
most people turning back. But Oprah kept her eye on her goal at all

times. Throughout her life she kept focused on the outcome, rather than dwelling on setbacks. An inspiration for social change, Oprah has shown that she has learned to love herself. Now she is teaching others to do the same.

Whenever I meet successful people, people who have achieved wonderful things, they invariably tell me it all started with an idea, something they were striving towards. I don't believe in coincidence or in being in the right place at the right time. I believe we need to make our own luck. I will not accept *no* and I will not accept *second best*.

How do you get to that place? By setting goals. Everyone has to have a goal in life, something to aspire to. By setting goals we are creating our future. Goals create our purpose in life. Goals give us a sense of purpose. Goals provide us with a focus.

By concentrating all our energy and thoughts we achieve immediate results. A more modern day guru puts it like this:

> *'A lot of people are afraid to say what they want.*
> *That's why they don't get what they want'*
>
> Madonna

Goals are all about living in the NOW. But they are also about planning for the future. Goals are not cast in stone. Goals evolve. They're revisited and revised constantly in order for us to move forward. By setting your goals, you move beyond self-doubt. Goals help us to think in a more positive way, which leads to greater success. Success breeds better self-esteem and more confidence. Goals help us filter out the unimportant. Goals help us overcome our fears. Goals increase our motivation. Goals help us challenge ourselves.

Goals help when we're struggling with circumstances beyond our control. Everyone has days when things don't go according to plan. Everyone has bad days. It's how we cope with negative experiences that count. The key is what we do then. Less-than-hoped-for exam results should never be seen as a failure.

They help us acknowledge that we've either disliked the subject or not studied for it, or else that we didn't understand the material in the first place. If you admit that you tried your best on the day with the knowledge you had, then you release your inner stress.

You should move on to something you do like! Set a different goal. Don't let pride force you to keep battling at something for which you have little aptitude. Know your strengths and work with them.

You have to have the right goal. Are you focusing your energies in the right direction? Don't fall into the trap of having unrealistic dreams. Set yourself small, easy steps that will take you on your way to success. Whether it's learning a skill, further education, re-training, networking, set out to learn and grow. We all have to move with the times, keep up to date with new technology. We don't always need to know how it works. Not everyone who drives a car knows how it works.

Goals must be *long term* in order for you to set a clear focus. What do you want to do with your life? *Short term*, to show you how to move forward on a daily basis. *Realistic. Achievable*, in order for you to recognise your success. *Flexible*, as life constantly changes. Growth attracts new opportunities. *Measurable*, so you can set deadlines. Your goals must be for you, not for anyone else.

Goals must be written down in order for the universe to see and for you to fully feel. When we set our goal we need to give it time to happen.

Here's two great ways to keep your goals achievable! First let's talk about setting S.M.A.R.T. goals:

Specific Measurable Attainable Realistic Time

Goals must be Specific

We have to be *specific* when we set our goals. When we set a specific goal, as opposed to working towards a vague idea, it helps us to stay focused. We have to give ourselves clear instructions. Specific goal setting helps us define more clearly exactly what our goal is. Say you want to lose weight – how much weight do you want to lose? Write it down!

Goals must be measurable

Let's stay with weight loss. How long will it take you to achieve your goal? Who will help you? How will you know when you have reached the goal? Will you join a weight loss class and commit to going each week? Measure your progress steadily and stay on track.

Goals must be attainable

Goals that are set too high, or out of your reach will only bring disappointment. There is no point in setting yourself up for failure. You've decided how much weight to lose. Can you keep this target without feeling guilty or unhappy? Most goals are attainable if you set your mind to them and take steps to carry out your plan. Once you have identified your goal then you can begin to look at how you can achieve this.

Build in some flexibility when goal setting. Many things outside your control may make it impossible for you to achieve what you want. Running a championships race, you may develop ill health resulting in a poor performance. A sales rep may be well on target. He may work very hard, develop strategies, market his product well. But if there is an economic decline, no one will buy his cars. Be open to achieving your goal in different ways, ways that you might previously have dismissed.

Goals must be realistic

Goals are achieved by breaking them down, bit by bit. It wouldn't be a goal if everything was achieved instantly. We learn and grow as we continue our journey. Breaking goals down helps us to feel good, giving us the confidence and determination to go on to the next step. Don't try and lose the weight too quickly, for example. Being realistic is being true to yourself.

'Keep your eyes on the stars and your feet on the ground'
Theodore Roosevelt

Goals need a time frame

Unless we give ourselves a deadline we have no sense of urgency. Without it, we'll get bored and lose interest. We have no challenge to rise to. Think, *what is your time frame*? Weeks, Months? Make your goal achievable in that time. Do you have a special occasion coming up and want to lose weight? Then choose it, if it's realistic. The most important thing is to set a time frame and stick to it.

Here's another method of goal setting I've used in my own life to great success. When I decided to branch out and work on my own, establishing my own clinic, I knew I had several decisions to make.

Why I wanted to start working solo. Where I would work from. What treatment and training I would offer. Who could help me achieve my goal. When I wanted to open my business by.

Once I had established these things, and only then, could I start putting them in action to achieve those goals. Every day I did some action, however small, that would take me a step closer to achieving my goal. Making a phone call, networking with other people, giving talks to raise my profile…every day I achieved something that brought my goal closer. My timeframe was six months, a measurable, achievable time. I knew I could make it happen. Three months before my 'date', I had achieved everything I had set out to do. We must always remember to focus on our outcome. By taking small steps towards our goal then the dream we are creating will be achieved.

'Obstacles cannot crush me. Every obstacle yields to stern resolve. He who is fixed to a star does not change his mind'

Leonardo Da Vinci

You can use the same method. I'm going to use the example of weight loss to illustrate my point. If, for example, you want to lose weight then you set a focus on your goal by asking the following questions: WHAT do I want to achieve? WHY do I want to lose weight? WHO is going to help me achieve my goal? WHERE will I go to get help? WHEN will I be able to achieve this by?

Now you know how to set a goal, you have to decide what your goal is!

Remember I told you you'd find your path in this book? Well, this is where it happens.

'You can't rest unless you set goals that make you stretch'
Tom Hopkins

I want to give you a word of caution. Be careful what you wish for - wishes do come true. You can choose anything at all from life's menu. Just remember the cardinal rule – you can't ask to manifest money – it will never come directly. Of course you don't have to ask for material goods. They bring great responsibilities. We just have to look at a random selection of lotto millionaires to realise that money can't buy you happiness. But if you want to attract financial abundance ask Spirit for what will *manifest* money. It may come in the form of an opportunity which will bring a bigger pay cheque.

Visualisation and goal setting, when used together, are tremendous sources of power. They'll help you break free of the cocoon that's binding you, so you can enjoy the life that's waiting for you. Did you know that just before a butterfly breaks free of its cocoon, the chrysalis becomes completely clear? Let's get you there... Dream BIG, OK? It's TIME!

20

The Butterfly Blueprint
7 Steps To Your Dreams

1. WHAT IS YOUR VISION FOR YOUR LIFE?

We've talked about why we need goals and how to set them. Now it's crunch time! Time to get off the fence. It's time to decide what you want to *do* with your life. Ultimately your life's going to be in a holding pattern until you finally admit: What do *you* want?

What fulfils you and makes you smile? What do you want your life legacy to be? Dump all the excuses you've come up with so far. You have all the tools you need.

I need you to go to Spirit now and thank its energy for all the blessings in your life to date. Ask Spirit for help in making this powerful, mystical process real. Ask Spirit to give you all the answers you already know but were too afraid to voice till now.

It's not the outside that we are changing; it's the inside of us: the thoughts, emotions and feelings. When change happens, the outside takes care of itself. Something has happened within you already. There is a sparkle, a magic when someone really loves life and is truly happy. The Power is within each and every one of us. Once we unlock the habitual patterns to our thought process there is a whole big life waiting to be lived. Are you ready?

This is *your* life. No one person can change it except you. You have the techniques. You're more in control, feel better and think in a more positive way. Now it's time to take the next step. Really reach out and make those dreams come true. Don't waste your precious life. Look at yourself in the mirror right now and ask yourself, *What do I want?*

It's time to rewrite your wish list. A Rolls Royce? A new home?

Good health and happiness? The holiday you have always longed for? Do you want a new challenge? New opportunities? Do you want to help others? Give more of yourself? Do you want to get back into education? Leave your dead-end job? Improve your relationships? What do you want to achieve? Write down all the things you want to achieve in your lifetime.

The choices are endless. Still struggling to decide? Here's one of the quickest, most effective ways I know for finding out exactly what we want. Your findings may surprise you.

I'm a very visual person, so I find it quite hard to learn just by reading text. When I was training in clinical hypnosis, I came across Tony Buzan's wonderful book entitled 'Use Your Head' which describes learning through mind mapping. His ideas intrigued me.

Our brain thinks from an image centre and then radiates out. Walt Disney said of his achievements, 'It all started with an image'. In other words, our brain forms a picture. It remembers by imagination and association. For example, if you think of a sunset, your mind will see images, colours, not words. When I am rehearsing a talk I have certain images that trigger words in my mind. People are amazed to discover I don't even work from notes. It all comes from my heart, from the Power within me.

Something very powerful happens when we commit our dreams to paper. They come alive.

You've written *your* wish list. Use it now to create a map of your life. Turn to your *Butterfly Journal*. In the centre put your home. Sketch how you want it to look. It doesn't matter that you're not Rembrandt. Draw simple symbols representing those things you want it to include. Now draw paths leading off from it. You decide where those paths lead – to a new car, happiness, 'me' time, work, travel, holidays, new skills, relationships…the list is endless. You're limited only by your imagination.

Make it exciting; have smaller paths leading off main roads. Visualise challenges along the way. Make it adventurous, make it dangerous.

Give yourself opportunities to step out of your comfort zone. You are now controlling your life, so nothing bad can happen. Remember, you created your own fears and anxieties. This is a chance to control your negative thinking. You can change your perception of challenges - through acceptance, courage and self-relaxation. Make the map as colourful as you want. Make the journey as long – or as short – as you want it to be.

Create the map as an aid to focus. Make it as bright and exciting as you can. Choose colours and symbols that trigger ideas in you. They should represent the thoughts you want to retain or symbolise the hidden desires in your subconscious. There are no restrictions – no right or wrong way. Just do it!

2. WORK ON YOUR SELF

Now you know what you want, it's time to acknowledge your Self. What is unique about you? What good qualities do you have that are going to get you where you want to be? How are you going to achieve those dreams?

Keep working on yourself, using the self-relaxation and RED-X techniques I've taught you. As new issues crop up in your life, divest yourself of negative energies as they emerge. Remember how it feels to sandbag all those senseless resentments and feelings of frustration. Work on fear as it raises its ugly head, using the fear meditation in Caterpillar. Use mirror work to improve your self-esteem.

3. REFINE YOUR VISION

Use the goal setting techniques I taught you in Cocoon to make those dreams a reality. What steps do you need to take to start the process? Who can help you achieve your dreams? When do you want to achieve them by? Who are you going to ask to help you? How can you do more of the things you enjoy? Are your dreams realistic and achievable? Within your timeframe? Choose dreams you can work towards. Be true to yourself. Make a plan today and begin to turn your vision into reality.

145

Checklist

From your list, pick out the goal you know you can achieve first and put your energy into achieving it.

Write down why you want to achieve that goal.

Write down how you can help others by setting this goal. What will this goal achieve for you?

Set yourself a timeframe. Then make that first phone call and get into action.

Practice visualisation. What would it feel like to have achieved your goal? How would you look? Where would you be living? What would your friends say?

Do your self-relaxation each day along with your visualisation techniques, to strengthen your vision.

4. COMMIT TO YOUR SELF

Stop making excuses and start today. Think big and take the first steps now. You owe it to yourself. Set a time scale. Give it time to manifest and materialise. Trust that when you send the order out to the universe that the energy will begin to work right away. You will start to put the energy into action to make this happen. Commit to being your Highest Self. Use the Three C's in Caterpillar to get you there – Courage, Commitment and Control.

5. MODEL YOURSELF ON SUCCESSFUL PEOPLE

Look at who has already achieved success and find out how they did it. Look for a mentor who is willing to share with you how they achieved their goals. When the student is ready the teacher

146

will appear. I have never been let down. Don't be afraid to ask for help along the way.

6. REMEMBER, ACTION SPEAKS LOUDER THAN WORDS

When you take action you are moving in the direction of your dream. You decide – how long is your journey to be before you reach your dream and goals?

No matter how long it takes, keep focused on your goal. You have to *trust* that the universe will deliver your order at just the right time, Universal Time, not our time. Don't keep wondering when your wishes will manifest. When I 'ordered' my new home many things had to take place before the right home for me came on the market. The important thing to remember is you are moving one step nearer every day. You don't know when that day will come. But it will happen sooner if you have enough *desire,* if you *persevere*, if you stay *determined*, if you *trust* it will happen. Before long your order will be delivered. Everything happens in universal time, God's time. We just have to be patient.

7. CULTIVATE AN ATTITUDE OF GRATITUDE

Remember to thank your God for all things – the abundance in your life and all the lessons we receive daily.

There'll be more about that in the next section. You're about to master the challenges of life as a butterfly. Are you excited? Can you feel the sense of hope and new beginnings?

LEARNING TO FLY

21

The Butterfly Section

The moment when the butterfly frees itself of its chrysalis and emerges is magical. Treasure this moment. Think about how far you've come. This is the moment when we finally reject what's wrong in our lives – the way our colleague treats us, the poverty we're living in, perhaps even the abuse we've been a victim of. This is a beautiful moment of Awareness. This is the moment we become aware we are worthy of real love.

Think about all the emotions and healing that went into creating your Butterfly Blueprint. Living through that process, refining it. Wasn't it all worth it? To know what you finally want from life? More than that - to feel you deserve it? As you take this first flight, feel the magic. You *should* feel thrilled with all you've achieved. Enjoy that feeling. Be like the butterfly basking in the sunshine, allowing its wings to dry before it flies off to whatever adventures await it.

Spread your wings. You are a miracle of transformation, an ever-changing masterpiece. Commemorate this first bright flight into life's sunshine. I want you to find some way of celebrating your new freedom, in a way that's uniquely personal to yourself. And I want you to remember it. Every time you see a butterfly I want you to say a little prayer of thanks that you found the courage to emerge from your shell. To show the world the Real You.

I love the quote from Primo Levi that says 'we would not find butterflies so beautiful if they did not fly'. It's time to put everything you've learned to good use. Remember – this is not a one-off opportunity. The most wonderful aspect of *The Butterfly Experience* is that we can revisit sections of it time and time again. Retreat into the Cocoon if you need to feel safe or take time out to re-evaluate your life. Go back to Caterpillar if you feel you need more energy. And of course, the first stage should be revisited on a regular basis, because the work begins every day, inside all of us. We need to be reminded of what we have.

You've learned so much going through *The Butterfly Experience*. Now, it's time to start reaping the benefits of all the energy you've invested.

> *'Just living is not enough,' said the butterfly, 'one must have sunshine, freedom and a little flower'*
>
> Hans Christian Anderson

This Butterfly Section is where we capitalise on what we've learned, and begin to reap the benefits of all that hard work. Above all, we use this section to see where we can learn to adapt our newfound skills to life. Adaptation is the key to survival. It's time to move forward. It's time to create your own opportunities. It's time to fly…

BREAKING FREE

> *'So, first of all, let me assert my firm belief that the only thing we have to fear is fear itself'*
>
> Franklin D. Roosevelt

If I'd told you at the start of *The Butterfly Experience* that some of you might be feeling a little fear right now, would you have joined me?

I remember hanging on to my mother's skirt, on the first day of school, terrified of what the day would bring. I knew I had to leave her, but I didn't want to. She represented safety, security. When we commit to buying our first home we're full of fear. Will we be able to afford it? Will we cope with the responsibility? At this stage of the process some of you will experience fear. The thought of staying safe and warm in the Cocoon is very appealing. Who knows what's waiting out there? It may seem easier today to stay in this place of safety.

But change is coming. Why not embrace it, commit to it, be in control as it happens? Otherwise you'll always be accepting second best. Besides – the best is yet to come!

By now you should be feeling calmer and lighter – you've shed so much. As we grow through this process we understand that the only way out is walking past our fear, out of our comfort zone and allowing ourselves to welcome change. Stepping out of our comfort zones – our first, dizzying flight as a butterfly – doesn't have to be fearful. We need to think in a different way. We need to see life as open, exciting. One of the most important tools for the emergent butterfly is *Awareness*. Knowing what's holding us back and working through those emotions.

Your life up until now has been fairly average or you wouldn't be reading *The Butterfly Experience*. Living as a butterfly means being filled with joy and happiness. It means being free to live your own life. No one can control you any more, tell you how you should feel. You are free to live your life any way you want. Yes, you can have it all.

My philosophy is you either work with The Laws of Life or you work against them. You can struggle and make yourself unwell. Or you can learn acceptance and use the skills *The Butterfly Experience* teaches. Life can be easy or as hard as you make it. *The Butterfly Experience* teaches that we are either controlling our lives or we are out of control. You decide.

When you think as a butterfly you think in a more positive, focused way. Your confidence is up and your body and health are much improved. You are more in control of your life. You have a sense of purpose. Now take a step at a time. One small, dizzying flight and then another. Relish the changes. Congratulations for sticking with me and learning the techniques along the way, for having the self-discipline. You are now seeing results on the final stage of your journey.

Now the hard work really begins for the butterfly. Every year as the leaves change and temperatures fall, butterflies travel thousands of miles, battling strong winds and flying over perilous landscapes to get to their wintering grounds – dealing with challenges. Even at this stage there are obstacles to overcome.

This section is going to show you how to deal with winds and weather – the knock backs of life. Even within the same breed of butterfly and within the same season, every butterfly has different experiences. The butterfly is going to teach you how to work with the laws of nature, exploiting the universe's tailwinds, if you like. You're going to learn how to exploit natural laws, in order to get the best out of any given situation.

Did you know that the adult butterfly's sight is so good it can travel over long distances, seeing clearly any dangers in its path? Now more than ever you're going to need a sense of vision. And you're going to need to focus.

22

The Importance Of Focused Concentration

'Concentration is the secret of strength'
Ralph Waldo Emerson

Focused concentration is the key to success. It is learning to quieten the mind and empty the mind of clutter. This is hard to do but with practice you soon will find yourself more content, happy and fulfilled. Do it right and you'll be free of stress.

When concentrating on any one thing, avoid tension in the body. Practise concentrating on different objects, for example, a colour, an orange far away and then close. Think of mountains far away and then of an object close to you. Think of a small object and then a large object. This will start to train the mind. I often start by imagining a closed water lily opening up. I focus on the flower to stop my mind from wandering. Sometimes I see water and colour; sometimes it's near and other times it's far away.

Practice, practice, practice. By practicing self-relaxation daily you are well on your way to emptying your mind of clutter. An empty mind allows you to concentrate on what you are doing. If you are meditating, focus on that alone.

When you are at work, focus totally on the tasks at hand. Don't allow your mind to wander. Bring it back to your object. It takes time and practice to train the mind but you'll soon see its benefits. By concentrating your mind your energy will increase.

The Dalai Lama says that if a person's mind is busy then he needs to meditate longer.

'All that we are is the result of what we have thought' Buddha

23

The Laws Of The Universe

Having an uncluttered mind allows us to focus on what we want. Just like the butterfly searching for nectar, you too can have the best in life. By keeping a positive attitude your life attracts opportunities. Did you know butterflies contain magnetic particles? Just like the butterfly we too are magnets – we attract and give off energy. That's because of...

THE LAW OF ATTRACTION

Like attracts like. Think about your friends, the kinship you share, how their lives run parallel to yours. What we think we attract. That's why we have partners or friends who are similar to ourselves.

The law of attraction applies in all circumstances. If you are consciously thinking about something you will attract that into the physical. There's a hook to this law – it applies equally to positive and negative manifestations. Don't think about what you don't want as that is what you'll create. By giving your thoughts to that energy you will attract it.

If we are feeling low, then we attract negative people like a magnet. Our energy is attracting someone of the same vibration. The good news is we can easily raise our vibrations by using self-relaxation. Regular daily practice has astonishing results - we attract happier partners, more positive friends and more opportunities. As you sow so you shall reap.

What we give out we get back. Again, it's all about spiritual responsibility. What have you done today to help another? Did you make life easier for your colleagues by having a positive attitude? Or did you send them running from you with a scowl? A smile costs nothing and goes a long way to healing wounds.

When we think and act in a positive manner then we rid our minds of negativity. Through positive thinking you become free of the ties that bind: anger, resentment, anxiety, guilt. The ties that hold you back from an abundant life.

Remember to work at creating positive things in life. Begin every day by ridding yourself of negative thinking by using the RED-X technique I told you about in Chapter 2.

Once we have decided on what we want to attract then we have to believe we will receive it *abundantly*.

LAW OF ABUNDANCE

'Reflect upon your blessings, of which every man has plenty, not on your past misfortunes, of which all men have some'
Charles Dickens

You've created your Butterfly Blueprint. Now I want you to take it to the next level. Imagine what it would be like to create unlimited abundance - health, wealth, prosperity, happiness. How it would feel to have everything you have ever dreamed of. Hold that thought, because I'm going to teach you the principles of abundance. But first, I want you to get a clearer understanding of what abundance means for *you*.

I recently met a successful businessman, a former rally driver, who told me he had once broken his back in three places. He would have been paralysed without the three steel plates doctors fitted in his spine. After the accident he faced a long and painful recovery. During his stay in hospital his family lost their home. He was too ill to be told. It was only when he came out of hospital that he realised what had happened.

In that moment he had a sudden, profound understanding of abundance. Homeless, he still had what was really important in life – his family. Through sheer determination and hard work he had created a successful business, but his family had suffered. He had been living life literally 'in the fast lane' and had forgotten what really mattered. Now he understood how close he had come to losing everything – not just through his accident. Since then he has never forgotten to be grateful for the blessings in his life.

TAKE A FEW MOMENTS TO THINK ABOUT WHAT ABUNDANCE MEANS TO YOU.

Abundance lies within each and every one of us. It's rooted in our perceptions. We all think if only we had a better job, more money, a shinier car, then we'd be happy. Please know this truth - we cannot achieve happiness through financial means. If we believe abundance lies outside our physical body we become stressed and physically ill in the search for it. The source of abundance lies within us.

Abundance isn't about things. Abundance is an attitude. Abundance is not something we can touch but rather something we feel deep inside. It's about recognising and experiencing real joy in our lives. Nothing stays the same, nothing. Buildings and houses are built and then they get knocked down, just the same as lives. We achieve great things and then something happens and we have to start all over again. The joy is in the building and achieving.

To create abundance, we need to abide by certain Universal Laws. When we flow with the universe, observing its principles, we receive more abundance than we could ever dream of. Most of us are too 'busy' to think about Universal Laws, let alone respect them. Ancient wisdom has become lost in our race to get ahead. Most people define abundance as working hard and making a lot of money, in order to buy more material goods. As a result they are overworked, exhausted. Our bodies suffer, we feel depressed, stressed and fearful. We get out of balance. Yet all the while each and every one of us has an unlimited supply of abundance in our lives.

A South African farmer, with a good piece of land and a good living, sold his property to go digging for diamonds. The claim he bought was useless; the farmer ended his life in penury. Back home, digging work had begun on his old farm. It unearthed the greatest diamonds the world had ever seen. The company that grew up around this untold wealth was named after the poor farmer who had abandoned his acres of diamonds in search of wealth. It's known today as De Beers.

I'm urging you today to search for the treasure within. Our sense of self-worth is nowhere more evident than in the limitations or

157

abundance of our thinking. You don't have to be a spiritual person, a religious person, or even a good person to find the wonders that are just waiting within you. Spirit doesn't discriminate. We all have the right to an abundant life, a life filled with happiness, love and fulfilment. But certain rules apply.

Am I willing to help others or just think of myself? What qualities do I want to be remembered for? Can I learn to forgive? Can I learn to let go of resentment and take control of my own life?

When we ask the above questions something deep within us starts to make us think. Neither do we have to wheel and deal to create abundance at the expense of others – that could never bring us fulfilment.

When we consciously start searching for the answers to these questions then something starts to shift internally – we begin to look within for the answers. They might not appear right away. Be patient.

Affirmation Rules To Help Create Your Abundance

Make sure you always say the affirmation in the present tense
Make sure your affirmations are positive
Make sure you say them with feeling
Make sure you say your affirmations each and every day

Here are some ideas to start you off, but it's infinitely better to use and develop your own:

I am overflowing with abundance
Everything I do in life is for the good of mankind
I am filled with positive energy
Everything is as it should be in life
I am free to live my life as I choose
I trust in the process of life
I am willing to be open to change
I am truly blessed with abundance
My bank account is overflowing with abundance
I am filled with divine energy and abundance

158

START TODAY AND CREATE YOUR BUTTERFLY
ABUNDANCE AFFIRMATIONS

If you follow your self-relaxation and positive thinking techniques then you will be able to achieve a higher percentage of abundance each day. Only you can do it.

MAKE A COMMITMENT NOW TO
CREATE AN ABUNDANT LIFE

1. Commit to the process every morning, by practicing self–relaxation for fifteen minutes.

2. Choose a part of your life, for example, health, career, family – in which you want to create abundance.

3. Once you have counted yourself down into your meditative state start creating your new life. Imagine that you already have the abundance you desire. Be aware of what it feels like.

4. Thank the universe for providing this abundance for you.

5. Your body will act as if it has already happened.

So many people fear that there is not enough to go round. I mentally go down to the ocean every day and fill my basket up with whatever I need for that day. No need to overflow the basket - I can always return tomorrow. For that day I may need energy to see me through a difficult day with patients. Other days it may be filling the basket up with clients. You choose what to fill your basket up with.

My life has been filled with so much abundance. I have three beautiful children - Iain, Jennifer and Calum - who bring me happiness every day of my life. I have a fabulous husband, Gordon, who is my rock. My mother and father taught me to be strong and always think big and believe that I could achieve anything. I've had the friendship, love and support of a wonderful sister, Rosemary, and her family. I have a beautiful home with a fabulous place of healing within it. I have the gift of friendship, amazing people who are always ready to help.

I have my health and am truly blessed with a wonderful gift of being able to help and heal others. This is my dream. I'm living it and I thank God every day for the abundance in my life.

THE KEY TO ABUNDANCE

Some of us are imprisoned in a jail of our own making. The bars around were erected by yourself and they consist only of fear. You have the power to set yourself free, to recreate your life. Love yourself, love others – this isn't a cliché, or a theory. It's the key to living an abundant, spiritual life. When you act and think this way, you send out a different message to the universe, and it repays you in kind. The Buddhists understand this – it's all about compassion. And it has to start with yourself.

You're not what you think you are. But what you think, you are! Look seriously at your life. Take time. Reflect on the past. Look at your daily behaviour, evaluate it honestly. Then ask yourself, how much abundance are you creating? How many acts of kindness have you performed today? Small deeds add up – together they create a happy life. Every day we add to this spiritual bank account, the abundance just keeps on multiplying. We give away then we receive. Begin to understand the spirit of this fundamental law, and see how it transforms your day-to-day living.

A patient shared his story with me recently. He had just been made redundant, had no money and was in debt. He went into his office and prayed fervently, holding on to his faith that something would change. Twenty minutes later he received a phone call offering him a job. He asked me if this was a coincidence. My response? 'There is no such thing.' My source of funding is simple. God is my source.

That said, I credit myself with the ability to make the abundance I desire become real. The converse also applies. How often do we hear about people winning the lottery and then blowing it, ending back at square one within a short time? Those people simply don't believe they deserve financial abundance.

Before we think about how to create financial abundance, let's look at this from a different perspective, to get you thinking. I'd like to remind you of the Philosophy of Enough. We all need money, its energy, to live and survive. But exactly how *much* money do we need? Most people's problems are rooted in this question. But how much of their anxiety about money is actually self-inflicted? People worry unnecessarily, feeling they must have the latest status symbol in order to feel good about themselves. But we all know that today's 42 inch television is tomorrow's debt. Wanting causes stress and stress leads to illness.

Have you actually really thought about how you choose to spend your money, what you spend it on? Some people choose to spend extravagant amounts on socialising, trying to drink their way to happiness. Some go on luxury holidays and buy fast cars or houses they can barely afford. Most households today require two incomes – two parents working outside the home – just to make ends meet. But what if all the unnecessary items we buy were taken out of the agenda? How much of our income do we spend on clothes and material goods to add to the façade, what we hope people think we are? We can only live in one home at a time, wear one outfit at a time.

It's a self-perpetuating nightmare of consumerism – once we buy into it it's extremely difficult to fight our way back to sanity. What are we trying to prove to ourselves? People try to divest themselves of stress with strenuous workouts. Why spend money going to the latest class at the gym in an effort to ease your stress? Keep your money in your pocket. Practice self-relaxation for a few moments in the day and you'll soon see the difference this crucial time makes.

> 'A man's life consisteth not in the abundance of things
> which he possesseth'
>
> Luke 12-15

It would be great if we got everything we asked for in life. If every desire, every goal, every wish came true. We would be so happy. Or would we? What would happen to our sense of purpose then? There

161

would be no striving? No sense of achievement after struggling to make something happen. Think of the hard work involved when we save for a holiday. The satisfaction you get from reaching your goal. The holiday – the fun and the laughter. Would it feel as good if you could have it all the time?

Without struggle you would be unable to grow spiritually and mentally. Life would become boring. If God allowed us to go through life without any difficulties we would be paralysed by apathy. We need obstacles in order to learn and grow.

A newly minted lottery winner thought all his problems were solved when he won the money. Instead he realised that having gotten rid of one set of problems he had discovered a whole new set.

Money is difficult for so many people. It causes dissension and bad feeling even amongst people who love each other. Hence the saying money is a curse, or the root of all evil. This is actually a misquote – the bible says the *love* of money is the root of all evil, a very subtle, very powerful difference. We dread being without it.

Financial insecurity, perceived or real, makes us grasping and fearful. By thinking 'Me, me, me!' and always taking from life, we reinforce our own fear, the feeling that we are not secure, not worthy.

The Law of Abundance tells us to act entirely differently. It tells us that when we give to the world, the universe rewards us. Again, the negative applies - if you give out nothing then don't be disappointed when you don't receive what makes you happy. When I spent time listening to the Dalai Lama he said that our path in life must be for the benefit of all. How can we enjoy wealth if we are surrounded by poverty? How can we achieve great things if we know we are hurting our fellows?

Give what you can without thought of reciprocity – that way everything is a blessing. The great philanthropists of the world, Andrew Carnegie and in more recent times Bill Gates, know that money is simply energy – we can't keep it to ourselves when there is so much want and need in the world. We have to give it away.

I have long understood this principle and seen it working in my life. As a result I have had many abundant rewards. Any time I have needed money to pay an unexpected bill, or to do something I really wanted that would enhance my spiritual well-being, I've received a letter or a phone call, a company asking me to give a training course perhaps, or more patients booking in.

If this principle works for me, it will work for you. You can ask for ways that you can create abundance, create a job for yourself, a promotion at work, a contract for your business that will in turn bring in improved finance. There is enough, more than enough for everyone. We only have to be open to one action: helping others.

Another name for the Law of Abundance is the Law of Manifestation. If you believe in your right to abundance then you will create it. *You deserve it.*

Are you sabotaging your ability to manifest abundance? Remember your belief system buried in your subconscious? What is it telling you? Do any of the ideas below strike a note with you?

- Money is the root of all evil
- Money doesn't bring happiness
- Money is scarce
- Rich people are stingy
- Money means problems

Whatever you've been programmed to think about money, you can change it. Money is not the problem – our attitude to it causes problems. When we start to understand that abundance is within each and every one of us then we can start to sow the seeds to create an abundant life.

When we set a clear intention, when we believe we deserve abundance, it manifests itself. Do you believe you deserve to be happy, wealthy and successful? If not, why not? What you believe you create. We miss out on so many opportunities in life by being negative. There will be times when we feel low, angry or sad, but we need to remember that *we* are causing those emotions through our negative thinking. We sometimes feel that life has dealt us a terrible blow, and can't understand the lesson we are meant to draw from it. But if we wait, believing that in time more will be revealed, then indeed more will be revealed. There is a whole big world waiting for us.

We just have to connect to Spirit. If only everyone could have this mindset, our universe would be a different place. It has to start somewhere, so let it start with you.

Louise Hay is a wonderful spiritual teacher who has created an abundant flow of wealth for herself and helped thousands of people all over the world. When Louise receives a bill through the post she writes her cheque and sends it back with love and openness. She says the company sent it knowing she could pay her bills. What a wonderful attitude to have. Why not send your cheques back with love and openness the next time, being grateful that you can afford to pay for it? And if you are struggling to pay it, try believing that the universe will provide it in some way and use that energy to seek a solution, rather than use the same energy worrying. Just watch and see what happens.

We all have daily choices to make that help us lead the kind of life we want. Some take the easy option and just allow life to pass them by. Some become angry and bitter, causing damage to themselves and those around them. But others choose joy, choose love. When we choose this path then we know we are working with universal law. Joy and peace enter your life unlike anything you've experienced before. When we start to help others something inside changes. Something magical happens when we reach out to other people. You are no longer alone. Because by choosing right thought and right action the energy within you helps you to do more. You will become calmer, more confident and more attractive to be around.

Now that you're working on attracting abundance, how are you going to make sure you stay on track – what are you going to use to help you navigate your way through this new life of yours? Even within the world of butterflies, different breeds have different approaches to the journey. What is your approach to be? That will depend on the LAW OF VIBRATION.

When something vibrates at a certain frequency, it resonates with and attracts things with the same frequency. Our thoughts and feelings are all energy and vibration. Music is a vibration, words are vibration. Thought transference works on the law of vibration – when we think thoughts and send them out to the universe, they are picked up by the correct vibration. Have you ever wondered why you sometimes think about a friend then the phone rings and it's them, thinking about you? Thoughts transfer. It's no coincidence. We often say someone is on the same wavelength as ourselves – that means they're on the same vibration. You automatically feel comfortable with that person, you speak the same language...

Your thoughts and feelings determine your vibration - which in turn determine who and what you attract. By really understanding this then we can attract so much more abundance into our lives. As you've read through this book, thoughts and feelings have been triggered, allowing you to attract the right energy to complete the work. Be on the look out for physical experiences – butterflies, tightness, which proceed negative situations. They act almost like a magnet, drawing the negative to us. Heed the message from your subconscious – avoid anything that makes you feel like that.

Prayer is vibration. When we send a prayer we are sending a spiritual connection. The Universe is always waiting. As soon as we connect to universal energy, we will immediately feel that energy vibrating around us. But unless we ask we won't get.

Be aware that negative thought vibrations can subconsciously sabotage your wish list to Spirit. Get to know your own mind. Always be vigilant against negative thoughts. Be your own spiritual detective. Avoid negative vibrations as much as possible – TV programmes, newspaper headlines, murders. Feed yourself only positive information. Be on your guard and never let it down.

When we are on our authentic paths, life events vibrate with us – we know instinctively if they are right or wrong for us. We avoid wrong speech, wrong action and wrong motivations because we understand the COSMIC LAW OF CAUSE AND EFFECT.

In other words why we should *'Do unto others as you would have them do unto you'*.

There can be few more ancient disciplines than the law of karma. As you grow in spirit, you begin to see the link between your thoughts, your actions and your reality. Any emotional discomfort or pain we experience is associated with Cause and Effect. If we are suffering it is because we have a karmic lesson to learn.

Many people fool themselves, thinking they can get away with hurting someone, but the universe always remembers. We will be forced to learn our lesson at some point. We all know stories of murderers or child rapists who have lived for decades believing they have escaped justice, until one day there is a knock on the door and they are taken into custody. No one escapes this cosmic law. Everything you do in life happens because you made it happen. Acknowledging that allows us to learn necessary lessons.

Another reason the butterfly stays on track is because it observes the LAW OF GRATITUDE.

We have so many blessings. It is important to remember that not everyone has them. So many people focus on what they don't have and forget what they do have. Think of the tramp in the street that doesn't have a bed or food. Be grateful for what you have and don't be greedy.

Gratitude never fails. Possibly more than any other attitude in life, being grateful will help your progress on your journey. It is important to thank the universe for all we have in life. We have to be thankful for our health, our homes, our food and our families. Are you grateful for the simplest things in life, the grass, the blue sky, the ocean and the flowers, the animals, the air we breathe? Are you thankful for your job, for the material blessings it brings? If you're at home, are you grateful for the roof over your head and for the time you have with your children?

We have to be grateful in all circumstances - for the things we have and the things we don't have. This life is a learning process, which allows you to expand. A Chinese folk tale demonstrates this principle. There was once a poor farmer, who possessed only one horse. When the horse ran away, all his neighbours felt sorry for him, but the farmer merely shrugged, refusing to rant or rail at the gods. The following day the horse returned, bringing with it a herd of wild horses, straight into the poor farmer's coral. His neighbours rejoiced and the farmer gave thanks. The next day his son was breaking in one of the horses and fell and broke his leg. All their neighbours said the horses were cursed; the farmer merely shrugged his shoulders. A week later, the Chinese army swept through the village, taking with it every young man fit to fight.

The farmer's son, with his broken leg, was left behind. And the farmer gave thanks, because he understood the LAW OF LOVE.

A life without love is no life at all. Love is the foundation of our lives. The love for your partner, the love for the newborn baby, the love you feel the moment you say 'I do', the love you feel for yourself. Love is all around us. Most of us don't think about love for one another. For some people choose to love animals, or the world we live in. By learning to love ourselves we can begin to love others.

'If you would be loved, love and be lovable'
Benjamin Franklin

Motivational guru Anthony Robbins is a prime example of this lesson. Someone helping him as a young man made a lasting impression on his life. He made his mind up at that moment that he would serve others. But out of a sense of love for them - not to cover his ego in glory. We don't all have his resources, but we can have his willingness. If everyone did one thing every day to help another the world would be a better place. When we start to help others then we are helping ourselves. When we give to others the universe gives to us.

'Loneliness and the feeling of being unwanted
is the most terrible poverty'
Mother Teresa

For spiritual well-being it is vital to consider what we can do to help others. Don't know where to start? Why not simply begin? Try smiling at someone you don't know. Often people are slightly bemused, but nine times out of ten they will return your smile. Just think of how good that person will feel and it will make you feel good too. There is a whole life waiting for you, don't delay your happiness. Start today.

Learning to accept people for who they are is a life skill – we can work at it. Human beings, like butterflies, come in lots of different varieties. Some are very controlling. Others are placid. Some are very shy, some are confident. Others are rude and arrogant. Learning how to cope with all types of people is important. More important is learning

167

to stand up for ourselves and to be able to say no.

So many people enjoy being the victim. Dealing with negative people can be very draining and it is vital that we protect ourselves from them. Don't be afraid to make a break with people whom I call 'energy vampires.' If someone is sapping you of strength it's better to end the friendship in as kind a way as possible. Just make sure they aren't reflecting your own energy!

I had a patient who came to see me with confidence issues. When we dug deeper into her story I discovered she had a relationship problem - with herself and her colleagues. They all 'ignored' her and as a result she didn't like them. I asked her why they didn't talk to her. Perhaps it was because she didn't speak to them? If we are unhappy with ourselves, we see ourselves reflected back in others.

Her colleagues were a mirror image of her own insecurities. I asked her to smile at every person in the office every day for the rest of the week. The following week she had to go a step further - smile and say hello. By the end of the first week a colleague had asked her to go to lunch. They realised as they talked that they had a lot in common. Mirror images of each other, you might say.

If we are dishonest we think others are too. If we gossip, we presume others talk about us too. When we become entangled with other people's negative talk then it rubs off on us. It is negative energy. What you give out you get back, so be careful what you say. Remember words are vibrations. They reach other people. Better use that energy to send kind thoughts to someone who's unwell.

People struggle with the idea that 'if you can spot it you've got it'- that we don't like our brash friend, because it reminds us of our own brashness. But a little honesty, a little humility will take us a long way here. Are you ready to put your hand up to the Truth?

I want you to think of someone you don't feel comfortable around. Ask yourself why. What is it about them that you don't like? Now ask yourself whether you have any of those traits? Chances are you don't like in others the same things you don't like about yourself. Learn to forgive and trust.

Take a minute to think about who your friends are. When we change ourselves then the relationship you have with others changes too. We seek in friendships our own values, boundaries, principles. On no account must we lower our standards.

It's very important to keep yourself grounded. I love to walk in nature – trees are full of positive energy. I often hug a tree to ground myself. People may laugh but it helps me get rid of other people's negative thoughts and feelings. Avoid them at all costs if they try and knock your confidence. What is it in their own lives that makes them bitter? Use them as an example of who you don't want to be.

A beautiful young woman I know struggled for many years with romantic relationships. Why? Because all through her childhood, her father's mantra was, 'Trust no one'.

We all bring baggage to relationships. Some more than others! *Inter-dependence* means being dependent on others for some needs. We have to work on our relationship with our self in order to have a healthy relationship with someone else. If we just believe that another person, pet or material possession will make us happy, then we are a victim.

We tend to fall back on co-dependent relationships because of a fear of being independent and learning to stand alone. *Co-dependence* means taking care of others at the expense of yourself. Does this ring bells with you? Some examples of co-dependency are feelings of guilt, or that you can never do enough, working too much, depression, feelings of isolation, perfectionism, having no clear boundaries, low self-esteem, constantly looking for approval from others, being unable to take any responsibility for your own actions.

Sound familiar? Then maybe it's time to make that relationship with yourself now before you can start any other relationship. Healthy Romantic Relationships should be neither interdependent, nor co-dependent. Relationships are something that need to be worked on. There is no magic wand. Whether it's a relationship with a friend, partner or husband/wife, the same principle applies. There is no such thing as living happily ever after, unless you invest in your relationship. You have to work at it.

A good book to read is *Catch Him and Keep Him* by Christian Carter. It's vital when starting a new relationship that we set boundaries. Remember the importance of your relationship with yourself. No matter what size or shape you are, you should treat yourself with respect and self worth and learn to nurture the relationship with yourself exactly as you are.

****

LESSONS WILL BE REPEATED UNTIL THEY HAVE BEEN LEARNED

We learn lessons from the day we are born. We never stop learning. Life is a wonderful journey. We all have chances, opportunities to achieve what we want. Yet whilst some seize those chances with both hands, wringing every bit of joy out of life, others take longer to learn life's lessons. They insist on doing things their way, instead of aligning themselves with the universe and its laws. Sometimes this has drastic consequences – people end up in prison, or tied in some other way that denies their freedom.

Until we learn our lessons we will keep repeating them. I used to try to please others. Until I learned that lesson, I kept coming into contact with people who were very controlling and wanted to bully me. Until I took responsibility for who I am and learned to say *no*, life was much harder. I suffered with my health. Saying *no* is difficult to begin with. But I assure you – with practice it gets easier.

Learn from the best. Never pass up an opportunity to add to your store of knowledge. And don't ignore the wisdom of the people around you. I learned many lessons in life from both my father and mother. They taught me to appreciate the good things in life and all that I had. My grandfather taught me self-discipline. Lessons like these are essential to our growth. But we cannot grow unless we learn to…

24

Live In The Now

Too many of us spend our lives thinking of the past. Enjoy the NOW. Stop worrying about what has passed. Take life's experiences and learn from them. Remember the good, and process the difficult times. Mulling over unhappy experiences stops us living in the Now. Think of it as driving a car, constantly looking in the rear view mirror. How are we to relish life's magic or be aware of positive experiences if we are holding on to the past? Holding on to traumas and sadness just creates more stress. The biggest culprit here is the ego. When we make the shift from seeing only the negative in others we begin to see the good in ourselves. We let go, releasing the negative and all the stress that goes with it. Change your thoughts! Accept only quality thinking. Make a point of using your mind to drive you forward in life and help you to be successful. It's about being willing. Are you ready to let go of your negative thoughts and really start a new way of life?

When we live in the NOW then we focus on what we are doing at this present time. Set your goals but remember to live for the NOW. It's the only healthy attitude that we can have. It's good to remember the good times but don't hold on to negative memories. The difficult times and the failures should be left in the past. They are just that. Past.

Learn from them. Don't repeat the mistakes. Remember, when we hold on to all that stress, tension, bitterness and anger it doesn't escape us. It will show up in our body at some stage of our life. The world is beautiful. But we are too caught up in the minutiae of life to fully appreciate its blessings. Too busy to stop and think of others, or ask how we could help keep our planet safe. The media constantly bombards us with images of airbrushed superstars with their airbrushed lifestyles.

The subtext of course is that this is how *we* are meant to look, how *we* are meant to live our lives.

With so much emphasis on the material, who has time to think about *who* we are, about expanding our spiritual lives, rather than wondering what we need to *have*? Newspaper headlines scream footballers' earnings. A few days later we see full-page spreads of their partners, spending £30,000 in a single shopping trip. Why does no one see the obscenity of it? Think what good that money could do in the third world. We are all guilty of excess to one degree or another. Why do we need possessions to make us feel good about ourselves? The same tabloid headlines tell us that money, fame and power are not always the route to peace of mind. Here in the West our basic survival needs are met. Yet we are more dissatisfied and unfulfilled than at any time. Our easy lives have bred selfishness. How often do you stop to think about where the world is headed? Or about your part in improving it? Everyone has a list of external must-haves like big houses, fancy cars, thinking that these things will guarantee us happiness. Yet at no time in history has our nation been more stressed or unhappy.

How many of us take time to really consider our lives? What has happened to the idea that each and every one of us is unique and important? That the differences between us should be cherished and respected? What about our health – our physical, mental and spiritual well-being? Why do we disrespect ourselves the way we do? Why do we reject who we are? There is a whole generation of women who have paid thousands of pounds to look like clones of each other. Plastic surgery is now an everyday event. But it only changes the 'us' the world sees. The only person who can change you – the *real* you, the one you wake up with at four o'clock in the morning, heart thumping – is YOU.

So few people seem to have the inner resources to cope, to rise above difficulties and cope with what life throws at them. We allow our negative thoughts to grow, allow them to cause us discomfort. What coping skills are we teaching our young people? In our culture today, it is accepted – almost expected – that the young will binge drink. Nightclubs are full of strangers, unable to speak to each other, flaunting their sexuality in primitive pre-mating rituals that would make cave men shudder in embarrassment. The growing rise in knife and gun crimes reflects a generation out of control. Why do our young people choose to drink and drug themselves into unconsciousness on a regular basis? Why is no one showing them a better way forward, a simple method they can use to control their lives? Why is no one teaching them the importance of a relationship with a Greater Reality?

For me a good relationship with myself begins by aligning myself with the Source of All. The world is made up of millions of different people of different temperaments, different skin tones and different cultures. We are all one in the world. We come from the same matter. We are all born of the same energy.

All over the world the unifying experience is praying to some kind of power. If we tune into it the way it wants us to, we all get the same results. Why wait for times of fear, anxiety and hopelessness to look to some greater energy for help? I have witnessed so many wonderful events over the years that I have no doubt about whether this Energy exists. I have always been helped in life when I have asked for it. In times of darkness there is always light. But we are sometimes so blinkered by the material world that we fail to see it.

No matter what has happened in our lives, it is never too late to begin again, to right our relationship or deepen our understanding of this Wonder.

A patient came to me to stop smoking. His body language told me he was not ready to stop; he was extremely stressed. I advised him to keep his money, and come back when he was ready, knowing he would return in time. He asked if I had time to speak with him, and asked me if I had a faith. 'It doesn't matter what I believe,' I said, 'tell me your story.'

Falteringly he began, saying he had recently been released from prison for committing a terrible crime. Though not religious, he had been praying for help, holding on to his faith that someone would look after him. Awaiting sentencing, while lying in his cell, he had watched an image of Jesus appear on the wall. He heard a voice saying, 'I'm going to let you go'. He looked around. There was no one there. When he looked back at the image, a picture of himself had appeared on the wall. The next day he appeared in court for sentencing. The judge said there was insufficient evidence and he was released. Faith comes to us in *unexpected ways*. If we seek it…

We are all energy. Deep within each and every one of us lies a beautiful spirit. Some people commit terrible crimes in life and they live with that knowledge forever. They have separated themselves from Spirit. We are not born bad or unloved. We create that person. And we can *change* who we are.

If you could walk away with one lesson from this book, my wish would be this: that today you take those blinkers off. That you see the light, become conscious of the Energy that is just waiting to help you. Let today be a new dawn. Start to build a relationship with yourself, with your inner self, your God self. Go within and find the cosmic force, the universal life energy that is your birthright. Whatever you call it, *use* it to help you in life. It will never fail you.

When we slow down and begin to listen to that small voice inside ourselves, we realise that Spirit is present in all aspects of our lives. In the here and now, it is present in all we do, in the people we meet and in the situations we find ourselves in. Time and time again people get an inkling of what's available. But unless we work at it, seek it out on a daily basis; what you experience won't be enough to really help you. We can't mothball it for a time in the future when we might need it. It has to be of the moment, found in the Now. Spirit gives us messages in so many different ways. We may speak to someone who gives us information we need. We may hear that song on the radio and a word jumps out. Universal energy works in many different ways.

Dreams are important too - we should take notice of them. I always keep a notebook and pen beside my bed to write any thoughts or words that come to me on awakening. Spirit comes to us in messages, spiritual postcards almost, in the form of intuition, gut feelings, insights or intuitive thoughts. By developing our awareness of them and, more importantly, following them on a daily basis, we empower ourselves, aligning ourselves to Spirit, to the laws of the Universe.

The ego comes up with all manner of excuses why we shouldn't believe this. Feeling threatened, it will justify any behaviour as long as it stops you going inside. It will allow you to devote time to overeating, binge drinking, watching TV. But it balks when you want to find fifteen minutes to tune into the Power that will turn your life around. The ego covets the flash car, the stylish lifestyle, but won't let you invest time to start your day right and organise your priorities. Fifteen minutes, to count your blessings and develop an attitude of gratitude for the blessings the day will bring. It all starts inside of you. You are the only one who can create your ideal life. You alone have the power within you. Anything else is a false dependence.

How do I know Spirit is real? Three months before my father's death, I had a vision. I awoke one night and saw the date of his death, and all the family at his funeral. I kept the details to myself but wrote them down. I knew I had been given this vision in order to be strong for my family. When the time came I prepared myself spiritually. I warned the people in my office that I wouldn't be in, that I would be with my father in the Southern General Hospital. My parents' house was closer to another hospital, but I knew he wouldn't be there. Mum phoned to say Dad had slipped into a coma. There were no ambulances available for their local hospital – he was being transferred. I knew from my vision what time to get there, so that I would have enough time to say goodbye.

When I arrived at the hospital, Dad was in bed number seven, a number I had clearly seen in my revelation and written down. We sat with my father for some time. Around 4.10am, a nurse saw changes in Dad's body, and warned that it was time. I knew that Dad would pass just after 5.30am. At exactly 5.30, Dad opened his eyes and looked down at the bottom of his bed. There I saw my father's spirit, as a young man, with dark hair and wearing a white, short-sleeved shirt. What a gift to see my gentle father making the transition to the hereafter. Several days later I described the moment to my mum. She told me of a photograph I had never seen, showing Dad just as I had described him.

Our sub-conscious awareness goes on. On the morning Dad died, I went home and wrote a eulogy for my father, naming the hymns I had been given in my vision. My dad had chosen the same hymns with my mother a few days before he died. At the funeral everyone wore exactly the outfits I had seen in my vision.

Life moved on. Believing I had to stay strong, I didn't allow myself to properly grieve my father's passing. It was a year before I properly went through the process. In the year it took me to realise how badly I was hurting myself, for some reason I didn't see any patients who had been bereaved.

It was only when I had began to grieve properly, that my books were suddenly full of patients stuck in grief. The universe knows what we can cope with. It was such a comfort to know that my father's spirit went on. I had great faith in the universe, which helped me get through, to finally accept that my wonderful father was gone. I knew that if I was grateful for my time with him, if I held on to all he had taught me and all the happy memories, he was only a thought away.

Be open to Spirit. We don't need to understand how it works; we just have to believe it does. Trying to understand it will accomplish nothing – intellectualising the process will only slow you down. To get past any doubts you must simply have...

25

Faith

'If ye have faith...nothing shall be impossible unto you'
(Matthew xvii, 20)

I believe that deep down in all of us there is a fundamental yearning
to be connected with the great Source. When we are desperate,
facing an operation, going for a job, or if a relative has committed a
terrible crime, at some stage of our lives, we all need to ask for help.
It's said that there are no atheists in foxholes. On my journey I have
studied and compared many different religions – and it's my belief
we all pray to the one energy. Faith in that energy is the basis of
all miracles.

But Faith is also a state of mind. To those of us who have it, it is
a *decision*. It is knowing that no matter what, things will work out,
that you are being taken care of, that when you find yourself in
a moment of darkness, there will always be a light that shines. I used
faith when I enrolled on my Clinical Hypnotherapy course, knowing
that I didn't have enough money to pay for the training. Due to
acute carpal tunnel syndrome, I had no job, no money coming in.
Faith allowed me to take the action, believing that Spirit would
provide. Within three months of starting my training I had
been given a scholarship. All my fees were paid. Faith allows us to
take chances, to welcome opportunities we would otherwise walk
away from.

Faith works, at all times and in all circumstances. The great
leaders of this world hold on to their own faith, and they never need
it more than in times of disaster. An example was the Asian Tsunami
of 2005. How quickly lives changed. At times like that we question
why these things happen. And what is our response? The twelve-

year-old who wrote his 'tsunami song' says that singing it still helps him and his friends handle the loss of their homes and loved ones. Without faith in a Higher Intelligence we have nothing. Events like that make us stronger people, pull us together, make us reassess what's important in life, make us revaluate our principles and beliefs. How important is our petty grudge when for someone else their world is falling apart? We're trying to be top dog, trying to find some elbow room at another's expense, then the TV screen shows us someone starving and dying. Time for a reality check.

We have to hold on to our Faith.

'Take the first step in faith. You don't have to see the whole staircase, just take the first step'

Martin Luther King Jr.

Faith is something that all of us exercise every day in our lives. When we drive our car and are driving down a steep hill, we have absolute *faith* in the brakes working. When we phone our friends or family abroad we just have *faith* that the phone will connect us. When we go to the doctors we have absolute *faith* in them that they will give us the right medication. We use *faith* every day of our lives and we don't realise it. People are too busy thinking that *faith* means religion. I also know what it feels like to fall victim to the experiences of debilitating fear, gut wrenching anxiety, temporary loss of hope, and waning *faith*. I've had problems in my own life, worries that I just thought there was no hope for. But in my hour of need, when I feared all was lost, I always kept my *faith*. It was the light that showed me the way and pulled me back to my belief and has never, ever let me down.

I know what challenges people have in life. I have had them and continue to have them. It's how we react to those challenges that shapes us.

Just know that no matter what is going on in your life, by holding on to your *faith,* the energy that we believe in whether that may be, God, Allah, Our Creator, the Universe, or other Universal life force energy no matter what we call it, good changes will happen. From darkness comes light.

'Faith is not something to grasp, it is a state to grow into'
Mahatma Gandhi

Every day new lives are born. Every day couples commit to each other in love and begin their life journey together. Life is what we make it. Life is for living. My own life has not been without bleak moments. My first husband was made redundant several times. Without my faith I would never have coped.

'If a man wishes to be sure of the road he treads on,
he must close his eyes and walk in the dark'
St. John of The Cross

When we ask for help, help will come. We all come from the same Source. I call it God, purely because of the way I feel when I think or say the word. I am not a religious person in a conventional sense, but I do believe there is an energy far greater than man's. When we do our self-relaxation we connect with the Divine presence within each and every one of us. I am in touch with my energy every day. I consult my energy, my intuition, and listen to the answers it gives me. By sharing this energy we can really help each other. Divine energy is ignored, disregarded, *wasted* every day. So many people aren't conscious of the divine energy within them.

The divine energy within me triggered me to write this book. I remain grateful to Spirit for the energy I have been given, for my healing abilities. I am in touch with them on a daily basis – I feel energy that others may only be vaguely aware of. That energy allows me to help others. Abundance for me is the God within.

When you are aligned with your 'God energy', abundance flows through every level of your existence. We know when we are without it - when we are out of balance we struggle. Everything seems to go wrong.

The exercises that I offer, opening the third eye through self-relaxation and visualisation, are not alternatives to conventional prayer, which is an entirely different experience. These are tools to help you access the life you deserve, to develop the same ability that I have, to tune into that Power. So many people have lost the ability to tune into that energy. What used to be passed down from generation to generation has to come now from a new source of knowledge. The Seekers among us have rediscovered these ancient channels to the Source. We've learned that it's not enough just to accept or reject the dogma handed down to us by others. We have to experiment with our spirituality until we find out what works for us. We have to look for inspiration from wise men and women who have gone before us.

As life progresses we have to move closer to the energy that creates us, otherwise we'll yearn for it always. But it's like a marriage or relationship – it requires constant maintenance. It's too easy just to walk away. When we instil discipline into our life, set goals and strive to achieve them, life becomes so much easier and more fulfilling. Positive thinking at root means having faith and belief in this benign power. By connecting to it we flourish.

There will always be the sceptics who need proof. For those of you who remain sceptical, the most inclusive thing I can say is, 'Just try it –what have you got to lose?' For twenty eight days open yourself up to Spirit. Take ten minutes morning and evening – allow Spirit in. It's only by experiencing Spirit that we know it to be true. It's already inside you. In any circumstance.

ILLNESS AND DESPAIR

Some people reading this book may have a terminal illness or disease. You may feel there is no way out in life. There is no hope. You can never be that butterfly. But you'd be wrong. You can be free from any pain or illness. You only have to be open to change. Yes, you may be ill but you don't need to be. You can alleviate much of the pain and suffering you're feeling by using the techniques in the book. Even now you can start learning how to improve your life.

By using the techniques in *The Butterfly Experience* you will start to learn to love yourself, respect yourself, feel worthy of who you are, not what you are. Love yourself for the way you look right now. Accept yourself. Once you can do that then your life will improve. I promise you. I have seen so many miracles in my life and in other people's lives that I have no hesitation in saying that anything is possible if you let it.

Start your journey now and allow that beautiful butterfly inside of you to emerge. Just think how free you will feel knowing you are in control of your life and that you can do anything you want.

GRIEF, LOSS AND MOURNING

People need strong affectionate bonds with other people for their emotional wellbeing. Death seems to permanently break that bond. I have worked with many patients who come to see me for bereavement. They describe their heart as sore and heavy, full of fear at the thought of facing life without their partner. Some people process their feelings by simply working harder. They try to forget their pain and sadness by shutting out the emotions they fear. It is very hard for us to accept, but the quickest route to healing is to accept the emotions as they come up. There is no point in fighting the way we feel - it is a process that we have to go through. I too have lost loved ones.

We have to accept that everything happens for a reason and continue on our own journey, hard though that is. We have to believe that when the grieving is over we will have become stronger. When we lose someone close it's vital we grieve the loss, have a period of mourning. We tend to withdraw from life. We retreat into our own world and our vibration is lowered. Some even turn away family and friends. We go through bouts of crying. These are all natural reactions – a process that has to be gone through in order for us to move on. It helps to hold on to the happy memories which help us let go of the pain. Bereavement is such a trauma to the body. Author Elisabeth Kübler-Ross advises us that there are five stages of grief: denial, anger, bargaining, depression and acceptance and we must go through them all.

Denial

181

When a loved one dies we can go into *denial*. I have personal experience of this – when my own father died I didn't cry. I just got on with my life. It wasn't till a year later that the grief finally crept up on me. I saw someone who was physically very like my father – the encounter blindsided me. The universe had decided that it was time for me to face what I had being trying to avoid. Pain. When we accept, there is no more denial. We have to work through it. But after the pain we are left with the love we had for that person. Love – and wonderful memories.

Anger

I was also very *angry* at myself. I had wanted to say so much to my father but didn't. Healing came when I realised that, although his physical body had left this earth, I could talk to him every day. Doing that has healed my pain.

Bargaining

We sometimes get into bargaining with God when we are in great pain. When we are grieving for a loved one we sometimes ask for God to take away our pain, promising Him something in return. Feeling the pain is part of the process. It tells us how much we miss them. Shows us how to value what lessons they taught us.

Depression

Sadness when we have lost someone we love is natural. It's normal to want to talk about your loved one, or to become upset when they are mentioned. Let your emotions out – expressing your sadness alleviates it, rather than making it worse. The support of family and friends is invaluable, especially around a month after a bereavement, when a reactive depression can set in. Don't fight it. But if you're still feeling depressed twelve months later, it's time to do something about it. Remember, there is no right way to grieve. Everyone does it differently. You do it the right way for you.

Acceptance

Acceptance involves coming to terms with the situation without feelings of hostility. It allows time for facing reality in a more constructive way. Acceptance is hard. We are out our comfort zones and feel isolated and alone. We get tired and weak and want time to heal. When we truly accept dying or loss then we can fully move on in our own life. It is the letting go that heals us.

One common definition of Grief Work is summarised by the acronym TEAR:

T = To accept the reality of the loss
E = Experience the pain of the loss
A = Adjust to the new environment without the lost object
R = Reinvest in the new reality

If you are suffering because of the loss of a loved one, a wonderful book to read is *On Death and Dying* by Elisabeth Kübler-Ross. Give yourself time. Society expects you to be back to normal after only a short while – they expect us to feel better when the shock of losing the person is really just hitting home. We sometimes need help. Don't be afraid to ask. When we don't we can go deeper within ourselves and feel very lonely.

Not only our emotions affect us. We experience physical symptoms too; lack of sleep, changes in appetite etc.

We all understand that death is a natural part of life's circle. If we could only celebrate that loss as freedom for the person who has died. If we could only hold on to the memories, all the wonderful times and store them in our sub-conscious. So many of us remain trapped in the past, wishing things were as they had been. Focus on the happy times you had with that person. Usually the loved ones we lose are old or have been suffering. It's heartbreaking when a child dies. But I believe every human being leaves this earth at their appointed time, when they have fulfilled their purpose on earth. We learn to heal our pain. Just like the butterfly, we can prepare over winter and emerge the following season to complete our predetermined task.

David's Story

David came to see me after being diagnosed with depression. His wife of many years had passed away and he felt there was no way forward. He had isolated himself, not wanting to go out or even see his family. Each day on rising he wallowed in his misery. He did the same things he and his wife had always done. He lived in the same house with all the memories. He ate just enough to stay alive. Each day was harder than the day before.

When he came to see me I realised David didn't have depression. What he had was a broken heart, a very different condition. We talked about the grief process, that whilst we were going through it bereavement felt like a long, dark tunnel. I told him he could choose to believe that there was light at the end of it. He told me all he could see was blackness. But there was light if he would open his heart to let it shine in. David had to remember that although his wife's life had ended, his was still to be lived. He had to learn to heal his wounds.

I taught him self-relaxation techniques, showed him how to think more positively. We talked together, looking at the ways he could still enjoy his life with his family, ways he could again feel wanted and loved. He started to think about moving - the house was too big for him, and it upset him, rattling around in the family home. He made up his mind to keep himself busy. He had been a sports coach, but had lost all joy in it. He began working as a coach again, looking out for young talent. He worked to keep the relationship with his family alive. Most of all, he was kind to himself.

The Secret Language of Healing by cardiologist Dr Mimi Guarneri is a wonderful book. In it she says, 'We feel with our hearts, we love with our hearts, we can die of a broken heart'. Something I have always believed. I know of a woman whose husband died after 57 years of marriage – she missed him so much she simply turned her face to the wall and died within a week. No illness, just a broken heart.

The medical profession has wakened up to the fact that it is not medication we need, it's a purpose in life. It helps us to remember that everyone experiences loss, and that there are people worse off than ourselves, children who lose parents for example. Make an effort to be outside in nature, let it lift your spirits. And talk with other family members. Remember happy times together.

'Turn your face to the sun and the shadows fall behind you'

Maori proverb

DIVORCE

Like bereavement, divorce is very painful. No matter how long you have spent with your partner, learning to live without them is very difficult. When I went through my own divorce I wanted to cleanse myself. I wanted to feel free, be a new person, to rid myself of the past and move on. I painted my house the week after my separation. I was so desperate to forget the way we were and make the house feel mine. Fruitless effort - I learned that no matter what I did to try and change the situation on the surface, I still felt the same way.

I had been married to this man for seven years. I couldn't just forget him overnight, no matter how much I wanted to. It took a year for me to shed a tear. That was when the real healing started. I learned to forgive and move on.

The pain of divorce sometimes seems unforgivable. We hold on to so much pain inside. We become bitter, hurt and angry. No matter how much you want it to happen, divorce is like bereavement. You go through an emotional roller coaster of highs and lows. I spoke earlier about words being vibrations. Sometimes we use language to wound each other. We say words we later regret.

Feelings are vibrations too. I felt very alone at times. There were days when I felt very low and scared but I always knew I had to find my inner strength to keep me going, especially as I had a young child. It's frightening to think that you have to survive on your own. Will you be able to pay the bills? Can you see to the needs of your children and still have a life for yourself? For me ending the marriage was a relief, yet for so many people it can bring so much pain, the shock of your husband or wife having an affair perhaps, or the rejection you feel, the dip in confidence you experience. You feel very vulnerable.

We feel rejected, sorry for ourselves, angry, bitter, hurt, unloved and unwanted. We have so many regrets. I had wanted to get divorced for a long time but didn't want to hurt family members. The one person I was hurting the most was myself. We try to protect our family but the one person we must protect first is our self. When we are in a good place then our family and children will know. Looking back now I can see that. I hold no bitterness and have moved on. I learned the lessons and today I use that experience to help others.

Reach out to others. Share how you are feeling, ask for support. Talking to ourselves in a positive way can help us through these sad times too. We can remember to be grateful for the lessons the person has taught us, the love they have shown.

I urge you, if you are feeling suicidal, or have lost any sense of joy or hope in life, go for help.

THE MOST IMPORTANT FACTOR IS THAT YOU MAKE THE DECISION TO BE HAPPY

A wonderful quote from a great book *The Monk Who Sold His Ferrari* by Robin Sharma reads 'No one ever on their death bed said I wish I had spent more time in the office'. Life is what you make it.

Butterflies need a safe place to hibernate over winter – I hope you use my techniques to find such a place in your life. It doesn't have to be flashy, if that makes you feel uncomfortable. Forget about keeping up with the Joneses. But make a home for yourself that is a safe harbour from life's storms. We all need a sense of belonging.

Today it's time to enjoy – to bask in the sunshine like the butterfly you are! Just for today live with joy, hope and happiness. Our fears are only illusions. Tomorrow is another day and we can start all over again.

Congratulations! You have achieved your goal. You've finished *The Butterfly Experience*.

You're ready to put it all into practice as you journey towards your abundant life. You can reread any section at your leisure. *The Butterfly Experience* has given you the tools that you can use for the rest of your life.

Don't dwell in the past. Live in the present. Seize every opportunity.

Your new life is waiting. Change today and you will change forever.

I have sent a wish out to the universe to ask that all who read *The Butterfly Experience* be touched by the hand of their God.

I wish you all as much fun and laughter on your journey as I've had. My journey goes on – wonderful things are happening in my life and today I have the courage to grab those chances with both hands.

Be strong, and have faith. Trust that you'll overcome any difficulty. Celebrate – this is the start of your new life.

Butterfly Journal

PART I – FINDING OUT WHO YOU ARE

Butterfly Affirmations (page 40):

Choose something that you are looking for in your life. Write three Butterfly Affirmations in relation to it, e.g. career, new home, family.

Date: _____07/10/08_____

Butterfly Affirmation:

1. I am Confident, Calm and Strong
2. I have a fulfilling, rewarding career
3. I have an abundant, loving home life

How you would feel if this was already manifest in your life?

Fantastic. fulfilled, grateful, happy
healthy and outward-looking
Confident and worry-free

EXERCISE ONE (page 41):

What does happiness mean to you? Write down a list of things that make you happy, e.g. spending time with family, enjoying your work, meeting a friend for lunch, holidays, reading your book.

_____

_____

_____

_____

Write down what you need to do to be happy:

_____
_____
_____
_____

EXERCISE TWO (page 41):

Write down seven things you want to change in your life for the better.
Don't miss anything out. Really think about what you want out of life.
Say these out loud and notice how your body reacts.

_____
_____
_____
_____

Now write down the things you need to change to make life better.

_____
_____
_____
_____

EXERCISE THREE (page 42):

Write down your gratitude list, all the good things in your life that you
are grateful for:

_____
_____
_____
_____

Now write down all the things you are good at:

_____
_____
_____
_____

What can you do to improve your life today?

_____

_____

_____

_____

EXERCISE FOUR (page 43):

Write down all the things you desire in your life. Don't leave anything out.

_____

_____

_____

_____

What can you do to achieve these things?

_____

_____

_____

_____

I am willing to be open to change.

Date: _____ Signature:_____

Now write down the things you wanted to do and to have in your life and you regret not doing.

_____

_____

_____

_____

How can you start achieving them?

_____

_____

_____

_____

EXERCISE FIVE (page 44):

Write down a list of your best qualities:

_____

_____

_____

_____

Now write down all the things you are good at:

_____

_____

_____

_____

What can you do to improve your life?

_____

_____

_____

_____

EXERCISE SIX (page 45)

Write down seven positive qualities about yourself. It's OK to repeat qualities from Exercise Five.

_____

_____

_____

_____

EXERCISE SEVEN (page 45):

Write down your Butterfly Affirmations for each of the categories you wanted to change, e.g. relationships, career.

_____

_____

_____

_____

CONTRACT:

I agree to make this the first day of accepting change in my life. I am willing to be open to change.

Date: _____ Signature: _____

PART III – GOING WITHIN

Chapter 15 - Cocooning (page 105):

Write what you consider success to be. Write down all the things that you think make people successful. Write down what makes you feel successful.

_____

_____

_____

_____

What could you do to improve your success?

_____

_____

_____

_____

Chapter 16 – Mirror Work (page 119):

Write down all the nice things you think about you body, e.g. thick, dark hair. Have a good look at yourself today.

_____
_____
_____
_____

Write down what you could do to improve your image, e.g. hair cut:

_____
_____
_____
_____

Chapter 19 - Goals (page 137):

Write down one goal that you want to achieve:

_____
_____
_____
_____

Write down how you are going to achieve that goal. Who will help you and when will you achieve it?

_____
_____
_____
_____

Chapter 20 – The Butterfly Blueprint (page 144):

Write down all the things you want to achieve in your life:

_____
_____
_____
_____

When are you going to start working on it?

_____

_____

_____

_____

Create your Butterfly Mind Map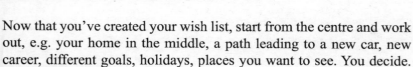

Now that you've created your wish list, start from the centre and work out, e.g. your home in the middle, a path leading to a new car, new career, different goals, holidays, places you want to see. You decide. You create your life.

You can colour this map. Make it as exciting as you want your life to be.

Acknowledgements

I would like to thank my mum and late dad for all their help and support throughout my life. Their wisdom guided me towards my path. I am forever grateful to my loving husband Gordon, my rock, and our children Iain, Jennifer and Calum (my Butterflies) who have always given me their continued support. Finally my thanks go to Anne Burhmann for her pre-publisher editing, encouragement and friendship.

Useful Website Addresses

Samaritans
www.samaritans.org

Alcoholics Anonymous
www.alcoholics-anonymous.org.uk

BUPA Health Care
www.bupa.com

Childline
www.childline.org.uk/Suicide.asp

KidsCharities UK
www.kidscharities.org
www.glasgowduckrace.org
www.blastfromthepastconcert.com

British Society of Clinical Hypnosis
www.bsch.org.uk

British Association of Counselling
www.bacp.co.uk

Cancer Care
www.cancerresearchuk.org

Holistic Cancer Centre
www.healingcancernaturally.com

People Against Cancer
www.peopleagainstcancer.com

Cosmic Ordering Guide
www.cosmicordering.net

Peacemasters
www.peacemasters.com